JOHN M. KRUMM

Modern Heresies

GREENWICH

CONNECTICUT

MCMLXI

ACKNOWLEDGMENTS

Grateful acknowledgment is made to the following publishers for permission to use copyrighted material from the titles listed:

ABINGDON PRESS—Herbert Butterfield, *Christianity, Diplomacy, and War*

HARPER AND BROTHERS—Julian Huxley, *Religion Without Revelation*

ALFRED A. KNOPF, INC.—Malcolm Bradbury, *Eating People Is Wrong*

MACMILLAN CO.—J. B. Phillips, *Letters to Young Churches*

OXFORD UNIVERSITY PRESS—Henry Bettenson, ed., *Documents of the Christian Church*

SPCK—C. K. Barrett, *The New Testament Background;* Moore and Cross, *Anglicanism*

UNIVERSITY OF CHICAGO PRESS—Paul Tillich, *Systematic Theology,* I

WESTMINSTER PRESS—Chadwick and Oulton, *Alexandrian Christianity*

Library of Congress Catalog Card Number: 61-5797

Design by Lewis F. White

Printed in the United States of America

335-161-C-5

To George and Dee

Preface

*T*ITLES cannot always be trusted. A clergyman I
know refuses to advertise his sermon titles in advance. If one is
ingenious enough to devise a really catchy title, he argues, the
sermon is apt to disappoint the hopes thus aroused. On the other
hand, a sober, descriptive title may sound so dull that people will
stay away. Much better, he thinks, to announce simply and mys-
teriously: "Sermon by the Rector." Perhaps the reader will think
that some such a course might have been followed with this book.
"Modern Heresies" sounds as if we purposed to pillory by name
the major perversions of Christianity which flourish today as modern cults and to denounce them roundly and warn the faithful
against their perils. That has not been the intention, and the
author apologizes for any betrayal of the readers' hopes. Our aim
has been rather to justify the fundamental notion of orthodoxy
and heresy and to show why some such distinction is inevitable
if one is to speak and think about Christianity in a way that does
not do violence to the fundamental Christian experience of salvation in Christ. To make orthodoxy reasonable and to show the
basic inconsistency involved in the major heresies of the faith,
especially as they appear in our own time, has been the author's

ambition. He hopes the reader will find this ambition an interesting one and will think the author has not wholly failed to realize it.

This book has been written in snatches of time taken from a busy life in a briskly-paced modern university. A sabbatical leave generously provided by Columbia University in the Fall of 1959 served only to produce an outline of the book and the first chapter. The final chapters were written without access to a library, and footnote references are therefore less frequent.

Gratitude must be expressed to A. R. Buckley, of the Seabury Press, who has advised, discussed, suggested, and then patiently waited for the results. My secretary, Mrs. Ercell Kullberg, has cheerfully and efficiently typed the manuscript in addition to her other heavy responsibilities and has even paid me the compliment of insisting she enjoyed it. What a way to warm an author's heart! My friends, the Reverend Doctor and Mrs. George W. Barrett, were kind enough to read over the early parts of the manuscript and to give suggestions and advice—but, most welcome of all, reassurance about the validity of the undertaking. They are not responsible, of course, for the contents except as a long friendship has put me in their debt in ways I no longer am able to identify. Much of the material here set down has appeared in sermons and has been used in a course in the Department of Religion of Columbia University called "Elements of Christianity." The congregations and classes who have listened as some of the arguments here set forth were first developed have helped more than they realize by questions and comments, and they too have the author's gratitude.

J. M. K.

London
September 10, 1960

Table of Contents

vii

Modern
Heresies

Christian Thinking

*I*T IS my purpose to write a popular book about a highly unpopular subject. The word "heresy" sounds harsh and unattractive on modern ears. If it is used at all, it generally has a half-humorous or sardonic meaning, as if no one in these enlightened days really took the idea seriously. Our image of the heretic of a former time—probably the setting is the Middle Ages, though we are not very clear about that—is of a sturdy and independent thinker who puts forward novel and "scientific" ideas only to be cruelly persecuted and suppressed by standpat dogmatists who lack the courage or the energy or the honesty to consider his evidence fairly and impartially. As G. K. Chesterton once pointed out, "The heretic is in many ways the hero of modern thought." He supposedly has been vindicated by the passage of time, and we applaud his courage and his farsightedness.

Nor is this understanding of the idea of heresy only a superstition of the uninformed. It is, if anything, even more firmly held among intellectuals. When Columbia University celebrated its bicentennial in 1954, coining as the motto, "Man's Right to Knowl-

edge and the Free Use Thereof," it published an attractive, illustrated booklet to dramatize its convictions. Included in the booklet
was an early woodcut of some ecclesiastical authorities burning the
books of Albigensian heretics. Plainly enough, this is the sort of
thing that Columbia University is against. The whole life of a
modern, liberal, enlightened university is predicated on the freest
possible inquiry and investigation. To take the idea of heresy seriously would seem to post "No Trespassing" signs on some of the
pathways of the human imagination. It seems to threaten the throt-
tling of new ideas and to suppress untested lines of argument. How
can anyone who has seen the progress that men have achieved by
pursuing such untried paths believe that any useful purpose would
be served by resurrecting the idea of heresy from the cemetery of
discredited ideas? So, to write a book, as we propose to do, on the
subject of heresy would seem to have only an antiquarian interest.

Heresy in Religion

The difficulty with the idea of heresy is even greater
if we consider heresy in the realm of religion—the sense in which
it is proposed to discuss it in this book. For if one probes a bit
further into the situation in contemporary intellectual circles, it is
clear that in some ways the idea of heresy is not altogether an unfamiliar one. An astronomer, for example, would regard the statement that the world is flat and not round as a kind of heresy. If
a student in an astronomy class insisted on affirming that particular heresy, he would be treated in ways not unlike the ways that
heretics were treated in the Christian Church (as we shall see
later, boiling them in oil was not the favorite method of dealing
with them). The Early Church banished heretics from the company of their fellows, declared their writings and their views a
menace to the pursuit of Christian truth, and urged that their books
and their writings be ignored by serious-minded believers. The
easiest way to accomplish the latter purpose was to burn their
books—although in a modern university it would appear almost as

efficacious simply to refuse to buy them for the library or to review them in scholarly journals! It is perfectly obvious to anyone who is acquainted with a modern academic community that some limits are set to the tolerance that serious scholars can extend to a man whose views are wildly divergent from those of the overwhelming majority of his fellows. So whether the word "heresy" is used or not, the kind of judgment it represents is being passed all the time in even the most liberal and enlightened intellectual circles.

But this judgment seems much more justified in an area where proof is readily available. The astronomer who insists that the world is flat and not spherical is stubbornly flying in the face of all kinds of evidence, like an eclipse of the moon or the flight of a jet liner around the world. The situation seems very different in the field of religion. How can one be proved wrong about such theological propositions as the nature of God or the ultimate destiny of man? It is one thing stubbornly to refuse to consider verifiable evidence, and surely it is quite another to hold peculiar views about matters which defy precise verification altogether. When we deal, as we do in religion, with fundamental mysteries about which no man can be anything like absolutely certain, is there not an obligation to tolerance and the broadest kind of inclusiveness, which there may be good reason for not urging in an astronomy class? In other words, instead of heresy being a familiar idea in religion and wholly out of place in science, may it not really be just the other way around? The last place where dogmatism and the definition of heresy are appropriate would seem to be the Church. Yet that is precisely where the ideas of orthodoxy and heresy have been taken most seriously.

Heresy and Freedom

Furthermore the idea of heresy seems to threaten one of our most cherished freedoms—the freedom of religion. Many people who stoutly defend the idea of freedom of religion assume that religion has to do with a sacred, private area of experience into which outsiders almost by definition can have no right to intrude. Again a comparison and contrast may usefully be drawn with our attitude toward scientific beliefs. A man is not to be allowed freedom to practice unorthodox chemistry in a university laboratory. The plain reason is that heresy in such a situation has calamitous consequences. Religion seems to many people to be a very different matter. Religion has to do with things which, although important in some perspective, are not usually from the point of view of society either plainly advantageous or obviously calamitous. It is concluded, therefore, that although we properly set a great many restrictions on a man's practice of unorthodox chemistry, none ought to be set on his practice of unorthodox religion. Of course, there have been instances—one recalls the prohibition of polygamy among the Mormons as a condition of Utah's being admitted to the Union—in which religious opinion involved practices clearly offensive to the majority opinion, and as a result practices growing out of that opinion were suppressed. But the point is that such instances seem so much less frequent in religion than in other areas of life. What a man thinks about religion has ceased to make any difference—in the minds of most people—to his full and responsible membership in society. It is often argued, for example, that while a political candidate's convictions about foreign relations, taxation, economic development, and a hundred other matters may be legitimately inquired into and scrutinized critically, no one ought to ask questions about his creed. This frequently repeated observation suggests a rather special definition of religion. Religion is seen in this perspective as a private area of response and commitment that cannot be—and ought not to be—investigated, regulated, or controlled by any outsider or group of outsiders, be they church or state.

This conception of religion has a long and distinguished history in the life of western Christianity. It is presupposed in many types of Christian mysticism. For a mystic the significant thing about religion is a private and inward experience of communion or union with the Divine. This kind of experience and relationship can neither be guaranteed nor effectively prohibited by any agency or influence other than God and the human individual involved. As one wag has observed, "Mysticism begins in 'mist' and ends in 'schism.' " In other words, there is a tendency in mysticism toward separation from the group and a devaluation of patterns of conformity to the group. If a man understands religion primarily as a mystical experience, he is not likely to be conspicuous as a defender of orthodoxy and an enemy of heresy.

Much of this mystical understanding of religion entered into that movement in the Protestant Reformation which has variously been called the "Left Wing" of the Reformation, the "Sectarian" Reformation, the "Spiritual" or "Anabaptist" Reformation. Some of the leaders of this group, strongly opposed, of course, by Luther, Calvin, and the Anglican reformers, emphasized the individual relationship of each Christian believer to God without reference to the Church at all. Such a religious movement as that of the Quakers, for example, put its primary emphasis upon the illumination of the individual soul by the Holy Spirit of God, although, of course, as Quakerism developed, the illumination of the individual soul was to be matured and tempered by the experience of the illuminated community. It is this tradition in Protestantism to which modern Christianity owes in great measure the emphasis upon the sanctity of the individual conscience. It is not surprising, therefore, to find a Protestant theologian of this tradition writing about heresy as follows:

From the Catholic point of view Protestantism is identical with heresy. *And correctly so: for Protestantism stands for the prerogative of the individual.* This is the root of all "heresy" . . . the charge of heresy is rapidly becoming meaningless.[1]

So perhaps, more especially to American Christianity which has felt deeply the impact of this "Left Wing" or "Sectarian" Reformation tradition, heresy suggests a menacing threat to the very nature of religion itself.

[1] George Cross, "Heresy (Christian)" in *Encyclopedia of Religion and Ethics,* Vol. 6, pp. 614-622. (Italics mine.)

Heresy and the Church Today

The purpose of this book is to endeavor to show how many of the heresies of the past are still—some of them in deceptive disguise—plaguing the Church of today. But surely before we can embark on this enterprise, we must deal with the massive and very widespread prejudice against the whole idea of heresy which we have been noticing. What does it mean to "think straight" about religion? If we make a distinction between thinking straight and thinking distortedly about religion, how can we be sure we are not just representing the limited outlook and limited understanding of our own generation? Science has learned that the heresy of one generation may be the orthodoxy of the next. Copernicus and Galileo and Darwin are often cited as examples of how this may be so. Is this true in religion—and more particularly—in Christianity? Has time shown that the heretics of the past such as Arius, Pelagius, Donatus, and the others were right after all? And finally how does anyone have the right to dictate to another man what he shall think about religion? Is it not an area of such fundamental mystery, and is not the conscience such a sacred precinct of the self that the process of forcing men into patterns of religious thought—however much the majority may think them the "straight" patterns—is always and everywhere a deeply repugnant one? Until one answers questions like these, a book on heresy will not find a very ready hearing.

Historical View of Heresy

Perhaps it is worthwhile to begin by making it clear that a concern with right thinking has existed in Christianity from the very beginning. From the earliest records which we possess, that is to say, the New Testament, we can see at once that Christians always were alert to the dangers of what we would now call heresy. Nothing disturbed St. John or St. Paul more than what they called "false teachers." They spoke of them in the most alarmed and agitated way. They are described as "agents of satan," "seducers of men's minds," those "who make God a liar," "representatives of anti-Christ abroad in the world." The New Testament is not bothered much about atheism or agnosticism; it is profoundly bothered about heresy. Unlike people in our own time, the New Testament authors apparently assumed that some religious opinions and ideas would have the most catastrophic consequences. One of the best examples of this concern of theirs is the First Epistle of St. John. We shall have occasion later to see what the precise heresy was which St. John was discussing. The point here is that it has immediate and—for St. John—deeply serious consequences. Whatever wrong ideas were held by the heretics of whom he spoke, the results were obvious—an indifference to moral effort, a depreciation of the sacraments, a refusal of fellowship with other Christians even to the point of withdrawing from the Church. This particular heresy appeared to St. John to be a virulent and deadly thing, so serious that it ought to be identified and shown up as deeply and terribly wrong.

This example makes it clear that heresy was always a highly practical sort of thing. Not every false religious idea was treated as seriously as St. John treated the heresy of the churches to whom he wrote. Indeed St. Paul makes it clear in his writing that he holds some ideas which he confesses are peculiarly his own, and he cannot claim any great authority for them. If anyone wants to refute them, he is at liberty to try to do so, and the Christian faith and life are by no means at stake in the discussion. One of the surprising things to many people is how few heresies there really have been in the history of the Church. Even today there are a great many religious opinions and ideas current which have never been, and probably never will need to be, defined as heresy. The author was once at some pains in one of his congregations to refute the teachings of a group known as British Israel. For the benefit of the uninitiated, it ought to be said that British Israel is the theory that the British nation (and America, too, by derivation)

represents the descendants of the ten lost tribes of the children of
Israel. This proposition is supported by such triumphantly logical
proofs as that the name "Saxon" can be seen to be derived from
the words "Isaac's son"! The views of British Israel are in the
opinion of most Christians, I suppose, patently false. It is not
likely, however, that any church council now or in the future will
formally declare them to be heretical. They are not so much heretical as irrelevant. They do not deal with matters of fundamental
importance. They do not have any very obvious immediate consequences of a grave and serious sort. They can probably be safely
tolerated within the broad family of the Christian Church, though
one may have his reservations about the wisdom and sagacity of
their adherents.

Heresies Have Consequences

The idea of heresy assumes then that *some* opinions
in religion have serious consequences. That is a proposition which
does not command universal assent. There is a venerable cliché to
the effect that what a man believes is not so important as what he
does. Now that is true if one means that a mere intellectual opinion
which has no consequences in fundamental attitude or behavior is
not to be taken seriously. What the cliché overlooks is that for the
most part a man's attitude and behavior depend very largely on
what he believes most deeply and passionately. Again it is G. K.
Chesterton who points out that a landlady, considering whether to
rent a room to a prospective lodger, will be very much concerned
indeed with what that man believes. She is not so much concerned, says Chesterton, with what he has in his pocket as with
what he has in his heart. He may have ample money in his pocket,
but if he does not in his heart believe in honesty and integrity,
then the landlady will have made a poor bargain. From her point of
view, the belief that it is all right to skip out without paying one's
rent is a deeply serious heresy. It is dangerous precisely because it

undermines the whole basis of respect and dependability on which the relationship of landlord and tenant must rest.

Every society—indeed every sort of human relationship—has such subversive heresies, that is to say, attitudes or convictions which break down the relationship and annul it. The life of a modern university has a number of such heresies. One example is the belief that it is right to trim the facts to fit one's own theories. One of the reasons, I suspect, why Communists are regarded with suspicion as possible teachers in our universities and colleges is the supposition—whether justified or not, I do not say—that they are committed to just such a "heresy" as this. A man can be wrong about his facts; he can be the unconscious victim of a desire to have the facts come out in the way which supports his theory. All that, while deplorable, is to be tolerated within limits—for who is not guilty of it in some way or another? But if a man believes that he *ought* to suppress or distort the facts in favor of some theory or point of view, then he is clearly guilty of a fundamental academic heresy, since integrity and a willingness to sit down in reverence before facts—as someone has put it—are among the foundation stones of any reputable academic community.

For the most part the Christian Church in its efforts to define heresy has not been motivated by an ambition to hunt down and root out every unpopular doctrine it can lay its hands on. Heresy hunting may, of course, get out of control, but for the most part the Church has been willing to tolerate a great many erratic opinions about its faith with a rather remarkable degree of equanimity. But if a man persists in holding and teaching a belief which undermines and destroys the fundamental Christian outlook and attitude, then the Church is obliged to identify and point out the seriousness of what he is doing, to warn others against it, and to withdraw its recognition of him as being in any way a representative or qualified spokesman for the Christian faith. This process takes a long time and much reflection and wide consultation among the members of the Church, and it is never the prerogative of a single individual. Indeed the definition of heresy has usually required nothing less than a world-wide council, meeting with sufficient time to debate and discuss the suspected views at great length. Individual Christians may, of course, give a personal opinion about whether any position is heretical or not, but it ought to be understood that he speaks only tentatively and with the modest recognition that his own convictions may not turn out to be those which the Church as a whole will support.

The Problems of Theological Language

A further question, however, is how one can possibly be so precise in his use of theological language that distinctions can be made between orthodox and heretical ways of talking. Isn't the attempt to describe God so impossible that almost any language is as adequate—or as inadequate—as any other? Up against a vast and fathomless mystery such as the nature of the Divine, how are we warranted in making such a fuss about precisely how one speaks of it?

It has long been recognized by reputable theologians that the language of theology poses very special difficulties. As long ago as the end of the second century, Clement of Alexandria wrote about this troublesome matter:

This discourse respecting God is most difficult to handle. For since the first principle of everything is difficult to find out, the absolutely first and oldest principle, which is the cause of all other things being and having been, is difficult to exhibit. For how can that be expressed which is neither genus, nor difference, nor species, nor individual, nor number; nay more, is neither an event, nor that to which an event happens? No one can rightly express him wholly. . . . And if we name it, we do not do so properly, terming it either the One, or the Good, or Mind, or Absolute Being, or Father, or God, or Creator, or Lord. We speak not as supplying his name; but for want we use good names, in order that the mind may have these as points of support, so as not to err in other respects. For each one by itself does not express God; but all together are indicative of the power of the Omnipotent. For predicates are expressed either from what belongs to things themselves, or from their mutual relation. But none of these are admissible in reference to God. Nor any more is he apprehended by the science of demonstration. For it depends on primary and better known principles. But there is nothing antecedent to the Unbegotten.[2]

The same modest disclaimer about the adequacy of theological language is found in the Anglican divine Richard Hooker, writing at about the end of the sixteenth century:

Dangerous it were for the feeble brain of man to wade too far into the doings of the Most High, whom although to know be life, and joy to make mention of his name, yet our soundest knowledge is to know that we know him not as indeed he is, neither can know him; and our safest eloquence concerning him is our silence, when we confess without confession that his glory is inexplicable, his greatness above our capacity and reach. He is above and we upon earth; therefore it behoveth our words to be wary and few.[3]

Despite his praise of silence, Hooker goes on to write eight books of the *Laws of Ecclesiastical Polity,* proving that theological modesty isn't perhaps to be taken at face value! But although he writes a great deal of theology, Hooker is in the main tradition of Christian theological thinking when he confesses the shortcomings of language as an instrument of theological truth.

One solution of this dilemma is to employ only words that have primarily a negative meaning, that is to say, words which announce in effect that our human ways of thinking do not apply to God. Many of the words traditionally used to describe God are of this type. "Infinite" means "without limits." Man knows nothing in his ordinary experience of a thing which has no limits. Therefore, to say that God is infinite is to deny that he is like anything else we know. "Immense" means "without measurement" (not, as it has come to mean colloquially, "very large"). All things we see and know can be measured and to say that God is immense means, therefore, that he is unlike anything else in human experience. Much traditional theological language is intended to perform this

---

[2] *Stromata,* Book V, chapter xii.
[3] R. Hooker, *Laws of Ecclesiastical Polity,* I, ii, 2 and 3.

negative function—to strike down the limitations of human experience and knowledge in our conceptions of God and to say that in his essential Being he is the opposite of what we know by sense experience.

Not to realize the force of this theological tradition is in itself a kind of heresy. One might call it the Sunday School teacher's heresy, though Sunday School teachers are not to be blamed for the way they are obliged to speak. The difficulty is that Sunday School pupils grow up and never have a chance to correct this heresy which was necessary as a condition of speaking to them as children. The Sunday School teacher's heresy is that God is a great big man, identical with the bearded white-robed figure in the window of the church, or, as a misguided (theologically) Boy Scout leader was once heard to say, "He is the Great Scout Master of all good Scouts!" Against this both the Bible and philosophical theology would insist that God is not able to be conceived by man. He is high and lifted up, eternal, infinite, Ancient of Days, glorious beyond our imagining, ineffable, transcendent beyond all that we can know or think. "My ways are not your ways, neither are my thoughts your thoughts, saith the Lord."

But now we must look at another aspect of this problem of theological language. It can be stated this way: how can man serve and worship and love a God who is only to be described in negatives? To try to imagine such a God is obviously an impossibility; the result is what one philosophical theologian called "a kind of oblong blur." The religious spirit in man is not kindled into a flame of devout service and joyful praise by the image of an oblong blur. But this is not only a problem of human imagination. The Bible itself pictures God in such a way as almost to fall into the Sunday School teacher's heresy. He is a God who gets angry and then repents, who speaks and commands, who changes his mind, who punishes and then binds up wounds, who moves around, leaves the Temple, returns to it again, is like a father pitying his own children, like a husband dealing with an unfaithful wife. This way of talking and thinking about God—as what we sometimes call "a living God"—is the very heart of the Christian religion. Christians do not sing hymns or pray or give thanks to an abstraction, a God of negative qualities that remove him from the whole realm of human experience and human need. The God of religion is always a God who resembles man in important ways. To use a technical term, he is an anthropomorphic God, a God in the image of man.

The problem of theological language is a twofold one: how can God as described by negative philosophical language be anything but an abstraction; how can God as described in the language of prayer and worship and religious experience be anything but a superstition? It is the special burden of the Bible, however, to insist that God is both Pure Being and the Personal God and Father of his people. The Bible admittedly speaks most frequently in the latter way. There are, however, indications that the biblical writers are occasionally at pains to rescue their language from the peril of superstition by making it clear that the God of whom they speak in personal terms is the God who is above and beyond human definition and understanding. The famous passage in the book of Exodus where Moses asks God to tell him his name is an example. God does not have a name as men do, a definable character by which men can comprehend and understand him. "I am that I am" is the strange answer God gives Moses. Some scholars translate these words, "I shall be what I shall be." In either case, the meaning is clear. God cannot be bound or limited or defined or comprehended. He is beyond all the limitations of our thought. He eludes our attempts to predict his behavior and understand fully what he is up to.

The Method of Analogy

If the biblical effort to hold together what we might call the philosophical and the religious ways of speaking about God is to be successful, it must proceed by the method of analogy. Analogy is a useful way to describe what we do not know by comparing it with what we do and then using appropriate qualifications. An avocado is something like a ripe banana except it isn't sweet.

Hong Kong is like San Francisco except the climate is warmer. We use analogies all the time when we try to lead some friend to share an experience that he has not yet had by comparing it with an experience which he has already had. This is dangerous. Bananas are not much like avocados, nor is San Francisco much like Hong Kong. So the moment we make the analogy we must begin to qualify it with a long list of "excepts." So we say that God is something like a Father, except he is unchanging and all-wise in his love and care for us, and his love is never possessive and tyrannical, and he knows in a single moment of understanding all that we are or are to become. One could go on adding a great many more exceptions, all of them helping to make it clear the ways in which God is *not* like any human father anyone has ever known. Only with the use of exceptions—and this is what the negative language of philosophical theology amounts to—do we dare use analogy as a method of theological description.

A great deal of the criticism of theology in modern times is a result of not understanding at all this problem of theological language. Indeed, some of the critics seem determined to insist that the attempt to hold together—as the Bible and Christian thought have always done—the language of a personal God and the language of a God of philosophical speculation and Pure Being is an impossibility and that anyone who tries it is guilty of intellectual dishonesty and of perpetrating a fraud upon the religious public. Julian Huxley complains,

For theologians to claim that god is 'in reality' some abstract entity or depersonalized spiritual principle, while in practice their churches inculcate belief in a personal divinity who rules and judges, who demands worship and submission, who is capable of anger and forgiveness—that is plain intellectual dishonesty.[4]

Christian theology would have to plead in answer to such a charge that it is doing the best it can with the experiences and conceptions that man is obliged to deal with. The fact is that men sense the reality of a mind and purpose behind and within reality, and that

[4] *Religion Without Revelation*, p. 49.

mind and purpose can only mean something like personality. On the other hand, this mind and personality who is the absolute source of all reality cannot be a limited, finite thing but infinite and self-subsistent and so quite unlike any other mind or personality we know. The problem is not a real one for Mr. Huxley, for as we shall see in the next chapter, he doesn't think there is any mind or purpose in reality except as man imposes and realizes it. But Christian thought recognizes that most men live in such a way as to imply an objective mind and purpose in existence, and therefore they have to describe this experience as best they can.

What does this mean for our discussion of heresy? It means that since theology deals with words and statements that do not have any exact correspondence to the reality for which they stand, heresy and orthodoxy cannot be determined as simply as would be the case in the natural sciences. It is easier, as we have already seen, to detect and expose the heresy that the earth is flat than it is to expose the heresies of the Christian religion. But this does not mean that there is no such thing as heresy in theology, that is to say, that there is no such thing as a symbol or an analogy which is misleading and destructive of the Christian meaning of life. To say that God is a Father is only an analogy, but it is a better analogy than to say that he is a tyrant. The detection of heresy has as its purpose the discovery of the analogies and symbolic images which theologians use for divine realities which are so seriously misleading as to subvert the whole meaning of Christian faith and life. This is not as easy a task as the discovery of scientific heresies, but Christians at least think it is even more important.

Attitudes Toward Heresy

It is surely important to point out, however, that the legitimate alarm that a Christian may feel about a heresy that threatens to overthrow the whole Christian understanding of life does not at all involve or imply any lack of charity for the person who holds the heretical view. It is entirely possible, as Church history has certainly abundantly demonstrated, to be wholly orthodox in one's opinions and quite uncharitable in one's attitudes toward those outside the circle of orthodoxy. The converse is also true, namely, that it is entirely possible to be quite muddled, confused, and even dead wrong about one's theological views and to manifest genuine fruits of the Spirit. The problems of how to deal with heretics is a special problem in Christian ethics, but there is no justification for suspending the normal Christian rules of brotherly concern, sympathetic understanding, or what St. Paul calls "speaking the truth in love," in such a case. The use of coercion and, in extreme cases, capital punishment—sometimes of an exceptionally cruel sort —in cases of heresy has never been wholeheartedly accepted as a legitimate exercise of *church* discipline. Physical punishment and the death penalty for heresy were always carried out by the state. This may seem an hypocritical distinction to make, and yet behind it lies an important element in the Church's understanding of heresy. When after the conversion of Constantine in the fourth century, Christianity became the official religion of the Roman Empire, anything which threatened its integrity and unity became a matter of concern not only to the Church itself but to the civil state as well. To be a Christian heretic was considered as subversive of political order in the fifth century as being a Communist is considered subversive in the United States of America in the twentieth century.

The Heresy of Donatism

It was apparently St. Augustine, who first toyed with the dangerous idea that the state might properly intervene in matters of Christian heresy. The heresy in question was Donatism, a heresy about the nature of the Church which had been disturbing North African Christians for some time before Augustine undertook to deal with it. It ought to be noticed, however, that St. Augustine approved of the intervention of the state only for a very special reason. His claim was that the Donatists were forcibly prohibiting the orthodox Christians from enjoying the ministrations of their own clergy. The intervention of the state was simply to guarantee the rights of the orthodox against the oppressive tactics of the heretics. But whatever fine distinctions St. Augustine made, the dangerous idea was launched—heresy is the business of the state and ought to be subject to the state's coercive powers.

The story of how Christian conscience developed and became sensitive on the subject of the right of an individual to his religious beliefs is too long to recount here. Professor Roland H. Bainton has traced its tortuous course through the history of Christian thought.[5] What seems clear is that at the present time no major Christian body is prepared to invoke the power of the state—even if it were available—to punish heretical theological opinion. There are, regrettably, some countries where religious freedom is very far from being realized in any satisfactory way. Restrictions about publicity, education, marriage and divorce, and many other things related to religious faith and observance impede religious freedom in many countries. But no country in the Christian world today makes it a matter of government policy to inquire into a man's theological opinions and to punish him for them. Perhaps this is due in part to a general and widespread indifference to theological issues. In part it is due, no doubt, to the increasing diversification of religious groups—a marked feature of the American religious scene. But part of the reason is the growing Christian conviction about the essentially sacred character of a man's religious life and the recognition, which even St. Augustine shared, that coercion can do nothing to transform the inner convictions of a man's heart and mind. To take the idea of heresy seriously today will not be likely to lead to any alliance between dogmatism and political persecution. It can be chalked up as a permanent gain in Christian understanding that religious freedom is today widely valued and would be widely defended if any resurgent concern for theological orthodoxy were to threaten it.

The alternative, however, to boiling a heretic in oil is not to regard his heresy as unimportant or not needing refutation. Toler-

[5] Cf. R. H. Bainton, *The Travail of Religious Liberty* (New York: Harper & Bros., 1958).

ance is properly exercised toward persons—but not invariably toward ideas. There are some ideas that one does not want tolerated at all but vigorously repudiated and demolished. But the weapons employed must be consistent with the purposes sought in any such encounter. The Christian Church no longer—for the most part— thinks of theological opinion as the cement which holds a nation or a society together. Coercive and police measures are, therefore, not appropriate. But it does think of correct theological opinion—at least on some crucial and central issues—as indispensable for a full and rich Christian life, and so its weapons against heresy must be those which will reach and compel the inner being of the person affected. The war against heresy since it is a war against the fundamental convictions and assumptions of the deepest part of a man's life must employ weapons which will convince and persuade him to see in orthodoxy the more satisfying alternative to his heretical views. Not boiling oil but convincing and transforming ideas are the weapons of this Christian struggle.

This implies that there must be a very considerable amount of theological learning and discipline if there is to be any real encounter with heresy. For the most part, this generation is not so equipped. The line between heresy and orthodoxy is oftentimes a very, very thin one, indeed. Gibbon's famous jibe that only a diphthong separated the *Homo-ousion* and the *Homoi-ousion* parties in the later stages of the Arian controversy is a reminder of how narrow a path orthodoxy travels. There must be a cultivation of theological sense, a feeling for theological subtleties, an appreciation of shades of theological meaning. It is very doubtful whether these qualities of thought and imagination are sufficiently well-developed in the modern Church to permit of a widespread definition of modern heresies in an official way. There is, of course, a considerable revival of theological interest and writing. The Ecumenical Movement encourages perceptive theological discussion on a high level of church life. But it appears premature to press at the present time for theological definition of an official sort. Ecclesiastical officials are not, for the most part, selected in these days for their theological acumen but for their administrative ability. Although a theological revival is plainly underway, it has not advanced to the stage where authoritative formulae can be produced or intelligently discussed. We are in a situation not unlike the Church in the second or third centuries where vigorous theological conversation and discussion goes on but where the atmosphere is still that of experiment and trial and error and where not enough experience or maturity has accumulated to permit of general consensus. The pages that follow will have a great deal in them that is, therefore, tentative and debatable.

Heresy and Orthodoxy

There is no blueprint of orthodoxy against which one may measure the strange new shapes of modern theological discussion. The hymn which says, "New occasions teach new duties; time makes ancient good uncouth. They must upward still and onward who would keep abreast of truth," describes the conditions of theological orthodoxy. It is not some frozen pattern of words and phrases. Creeds have been amended in the past and may very well be further amended in the future. The real test of orthodoxy is not whether it conforms to the traditional forms of creedal affirmation but whether it is consistent with the fundamental Christian experience of salvation through the death and resurrection of Jesus Christ. There are many new and daring ways of describing that experience and of relating it to the rest of the complex of human experience. Novelty and heresy are by no means synonymous, Vincent of Lerins to the contrary notwithstanding.[6] Indeed the history of the definition of orthodoxy demonstrates that the heretics

---

[6] Vincent of Lerins, a monk of the fifth century, who in A.D. 434 wrote *The Commonitory,* the purpose of which was to answer the question: what is Catholic truth? His answer can be summarized from a passage in the work itself: "We hold to that which has been believed everywhere, always, and by all men." It is not always recognized that Vincent's chief object was an attack on the orthodoxy of the opinions of St. Augustine on original sin, freedom, and grace. (Cf. *Early Mediaeval Theology,* ed. Geo. E. McCracken and Allen Cabaniss, pp. 26-31.)

were often the reactionaries, unwilling to accept a newly coined phrase or a new way of stating the faith. Oftentimes the only way to preserve the faith is to cast it in new forms, to define it by means of new ways of speaking.

It is also oftentimes forgotten that the definition of heresy and orthodoxy is not so much the imposition of a precise formula as the prohibition of precise formulae. Theological definition moves forward oftentimes by the negative method of declaring what *cannot* be authoritatively taught rather than by offering a clear and consistent alternative. Orthodoxy is oftentimes not a precise line; it is rather a broadly fenced-in area of thought and expression. To be orthodox is to stay within certain limits. To be heretical is to stray outside those limits. The orthodox doctrines of Christianity are not intended to clear up all mystery and to offer blueprints of theological truth, clear and unambiguous in their meaning. If that is the image one has of orthodoxy, he might well read such a theologically unimpeachable statement as the Athanasian Creed.

Our Lord Jesus Christ the Son of God, is God and Man; God, of the Substance of the Father, begotten before the worlds; and Man, of the Substance of his Mother, born in the world; Perfect God, and Perfect Man: of a reasonable soul and human flesh subsisting. Equal to the Father, as touching his Godhead: and inferior to the Father, as touching his Manhood. Who although he be God and Man: yet he is not two, but one Christ.

Here is not a straightforward and instantly perceived picture of the Person of Christ. Here is truth which is paradoxical, many-sided, one aspect balancing off another. It is heresy, oftentimes, which is too simple, too clear, too precise. Heresy takes up one single aspect of a many-sided truth and carries it too far. The secret of orthodoxy is to hold together statements that, superficially at least, appear inconsistent. In this methodology, Christian orthodoxy parallels the methodology of modern science, which is more concerned to report experience fully than it is to achieve consistency. Orthodoxy is not so much a closing of the door to further enquiry as it is a fencing-in of the area within which fruitful and representative inquiry can take place.

Implicit in much that has already been said is the assumption that Christian thinking as well as Christian life takes place within a society, within the "company of all faithful people." Orthodoxy and heresy can only have meaning if we believe that the inevitable context of Christian experience is the Church. Those who understand Christianity primarily in individualistic ways will not, as we have seen, have any need for theological definition. But if truth is—as Christianity sees it to be—a social fact and a social experience, if Christianity is something to be shared, something to be communicated, something in which men find a deep relationship to one another, then the society must determine bounds of legitimacy. The Eastern Orthodox form of the Creed is in the first person plural: "WE believe . . ." The very conceptions of orthodoxy and heresy imply that my faith and my understanding must be balanced and corrected by what the whole company of faithful people throughout all ages have believed and understood. If some new definition of faith is proposed, it must be able to commend itself to the consensus of the Church at large. One of the difficulties of defining orthodoxy and heresy in our day is that the Church has no organs of community expression of a sufficiently world-wide scope to be trusted in this delicate and sensitive task. American Christianity is likely to have its own peculiar viewpoint; continental European Christianity will have a viewpoint which is substantially different. World-wide Anglicanism will reflect the particular outlook of the English mind, just as the world-wide Lutheran movement will bear the marks of the special religious experience of Martin Luther. One of the most urgent reasons for deeper ecumenical relationship is that the truth of Christianity may emerge more clearly into the light of precise expression.

Orthodoxy is the way the universal Church has found most adequate to express the Christian understanding of God and his relationship to man. This means that it will not always exactly correspond to the way you and I feel at any given moment. This fact

ought not to be felt as a burden but as an opportunity for deeper
personal understanding. Orthodoxy has the same sort of claim on
the thought and attention of the individual Christian as the body
of accepted scientific knowledge has on the thought and attention
of an individual scientist. The great doctrinal decisions of the
Church point an individual Christian toward some central implications of what it means to be a Christian. He may find the language
strange and unfamiliar. The issues being treated may not seem to
him immediately crucial or worth bothering about. Nevertheless,
orthodoxy certifies these things to be significant, and before an individual Christian or even a small group of individual Christians
abandon these formulae for better ones, there is an inescapable
obligation to probe deeply and listen sensitively and discuss widely.
A wise observer of modern popular religious discussion gives it as
his opinion that its major fault is, as he puts it, "a failure to read
the minutes of the previous meetings." A good deal of theological
water has gone over the ecclesiastical dam in the last 2000 years.
Because Christianity is an historical religion and a social religion
some acquaintance with that stream is an obligation. We turn to
some of the heresies of the past, not with a primarily antiquarian
interest, but in order that with the help of the whole company of
faithful men and women of all ages we may begin to mark out in
our time the area in which modern man can reflect usefully and
representatively on the meaning of his Christian faith.

CHAPTER TWO

To Be as Gods

*H*ERESIES have times and seasons. They bear a close relationship to the climate of opinion in the world which surrounds the Church and colors and influences her thinking and teaching. No heresy, perhaps, is absolutely new, unrelated to ideas and assumptions that have preceded it in the history of Christian thought, but there is at least one heresy which has never, before the modern era, been put forward so confidently and so positively. It is this: that man is the master of his own fate and the arbiter of his own destiny, the source of the meaning and purpose of his own life.

The modern imagination has been greatly stirred by the spectacle of man's power to manage and direct the energies of the physical world. In our own day, far from being discredited and discarded, science has been making even more breath-taking advances, reaching out even beyond the limits of the earth's atmosphere to measure and analyze and manipulate. What is more, ambitious claims are being made for what the so-called "behavioral sciences" can accomplish. Man may be able to control the processes of human motivation and emotional experience. It is not surprising, therefore, that it has occurred to modern man that even the fundamental meaning and purpose of existence and reality are his to determine, that, as a modern author has put it, "gods are creations of man, personalized representations of the forces of destiny, with their unity projected into them by human thought and imagination." [1]

Naturalistic Humanism

It would be fair to say that the prevailing mood on most modern liberal university campuses is this mood of naturalistic humanism. It is oftentimes explicitly avowed by teachers with a philosophical bent. It is even more often tacitly assumed or implied by the widespread neglect of any serious consideration of theistic religion. It is not limited in its appeal to men who can properly be called scientists. The prestige of science has created throughout our whole culture a veneration of man's skill and ability to control and determine his destiny. This veneration comes naturally, so that in our day when men ask what the future holds, the answer is automatically given in terms of what men may be expected to decide and to do about life. Toward the end of the Second World War a book appeared with the characteristically contemporary title: *The World We Want to Live In*. It is interesting to read such a book and see how little resemblance there is between the hopes of 1945 and the historic realities of 1945-1960. Despite these disappointments, the modern mood remains very largely unchastened, and the cry is heard in the land, especially at Commencement time, that we must be up and doing and make the world what we want it to be.

No one can deny the appeal that this summons has—and ought to have—to human beings. Christianity by its doctrine of man's creation in the image of God reinforces the general impression that man was made for responsibility. What he chooses makes an im-

---

[1] Julian Huxley, *Religion Without Revelation* (New York: Harper & Bros., 1957), p. 49.

portant difference in the world—both to him and to his society and to the future. The words of Jesus are sobering in their picture of human responsibility: "Ask, and it shall be given you; seek, and ye shall find; knock, and it shall be opened unto you." This means that man has in life what he most deeply seeks—and that is a terrifying as well as a bracing idea. The thing that defines human nature is man's self-consciousness about his actions and his decisions. He alone of all the animals pictures a future and plans and chooses in such a way as to bring it to pass. Christianity says that this deep-seated sense of responsibility is not an illusion. Man is called by God into a large area of self-determination. "Choose you this day," is a persistent theme of the Bible. But for the Bible this choice is not made in the dark, under an empty sky, against an impassive and neutral universe. To elevate man to the position where his choice and decision represent the only purpose and meaning which are to be found in the universe reminds the Christian of the myth of the Garden of Eden and the tempting words of the serpent, "Ye shall be as gods, determining good and evil."

Human Values

One of the major difficulties with this viewpoint is that it leaves unanswered the question as to precisely which human values are to be preferred, extolled, and expressed. A persuasive spokesman for this point of view has written, "There is not one meaning to life; there are as many as human invention and human imagination can dream of and find the ingenuity to realize." [2] But is it possible to maintain such a laissez-faire attitude in view of the sharply competitive "meanings" which today are struggling for supremacy? This amiable tolerance of any system of meaning which human invention and human ingenuity can develop and promote must surely stop short before the terrible destructiveness of Naziism or the stifling tyranny of Communism. Even within societies of a

[2] Irwin Edman, *The Uses of Philosophy*, ed. by Chas. Frankel (New York: Simon & Schuster, 1955), p. 186.

democratic and liberal sort, there are sharp tensions between competing systems of meaning. What can be said to reconcile the values of the Organization Man, for example, with those of the Beatnik? On the premise of naturalistic humanism the discovery of the inadequacies of either the Organization Man or the Beatnik set of values is simply a matter of experience. If they live long enough men will sense the limitations of their ideals and undertake the costly business of reconstructing them. Christianity would make a more direct attack on the problem. It would declare plainly and flatly that human values have already been described in the law and the prophets of Israel and incarnated in the person of Jesus Christ. The Organization Man is confronted with the ideal of individual freedom and personal integrity; the Beatnik is reminded of the responsibility any man bears to the social structures in which he lives, a responsibility that may include constructive reformation but cannot be content with nihilistic denunciation. The dogmatic humanist is right, of course, that since men were made for the kind of freedom and responsibility that is seen incarnate in Christ such an ideal will answer to something deep within them. They will find that Christ is indeed the true Light which lightens every man coming into the world. But this ideal needs dramatization, incarnation, demonstration.

Since most reflective naturalistic humanists are college professors of Philosophy, it is perhaps not surprising that the image of the ideal man turns out to be a kind of bland, disengaged intellectual, agnostic about all causes and commitments (or almost all), urbane, civilized, decent, a little tired and disillusioned. Such an ideal has been pictured in a recent novel, whose hero is a well-meaning professor of English at a Midlands university in England:

One was, now, a humanist, neither Christian or communist any more, but in some vague, unstable, central place—a humanist, yes, but not one of those who supposes that man is good or progress attractive. One has no firm affiliations—political, religious, or moral—but lies outside it all. One sees new projects tried, new cases put, and reflects on them, distrusts them, is not surprised when they don't work, and is doubtful if they seem to. A tired sophistication runs up and down one's spine;

one has seen everything tried and seen it fail . . . One is at the end of the tradition of human experience, where everything has been tried and no one way shows itself as perceptibly better than another. Groping into the corners of one's benevolence, one likes this good soul, that dear woman, but despairs of the group or the race. For the mass of men there is not too much to be said or done; you can't make a silk purse out of a sow's ear.[3]

What does naturalistic humanism have to say to someone who no longer likes human beings very much or believes that what they are up to is either very important or very reliable? The number of such people seems to be increasing in our Western culture. Even those who still believe in something seem curiously passionless about it, gently cynical even about their own idealism, pursuing a life of quiet and moderate pleasures but missing what Pascal called "the grandeur and the misery of man." Of course, as it must to all men, risky adventures and chancy encounters happen to such people. They fall in love, they get married, they bear and rear children, they make friends, they taste disappointment and face discouragement, they know illness and infirmity, and finally they face the fact of death. In all this they are likely to live far more fully than their philosophy would lead one to expect and to depend upon meanings which they make no room for in their speculations. As it appears to Christian believers, such men draw at such times upon the spiritual reserves of the great Christian tradition about the meaning and purpose of life. The fact that they owe more to it than they have put into it is lost on most of them, at least until it is too late.

The Purposes of God

There is another disadvantage to the view that man is the source of the values of life, and that is that it puts a premium on the arts of manipulation. If man is at the apex of reality, then

[3] Malcolm Bradbury, *Eating People Is Wrong.* (New York: Alfred Knopf, 1960.)

he will look upon it as something to be exploited, employed, managed, and used for his benefit and pleasure. It is difficult to define the precise point at which this tendency becomes "heretical." In its origin and essence, and expressed within limits, this determination is rooted in the command of Genesis to replenish the earth and subdue it (Genesis 1:28). Indeed, it can be argued that this picture of man as the controller of creation is the charter of scientific endeavor. Evidence may be cited that the full development of scientific undertaking has been limited to those countries and cultures where the biblical doctrine of creation is taken seriously (that is to say, where Islam and the Judaeo-Christian traditions have exerted influence). What has already been said about the Christian summons to responsibility includes the obligation to manage life in ways that are consistent with the purposes of God.

If we assume, however, that there are no such things as "purposes of God," then man appears to be at liberty to make of life anything he wants to. Nature is regarded as something to be exploited rather than, as in Christian sacramentalism, something to be redeemed and seen as a vehicle of God's grace and power. Life is not something to be trusted in any fundamental sense, but something to be managed. And the final and most serious step of all, one's fellow man is almost unconsciously brought within the domain of that which is to be manipulated for purposes which someone— probably I—think best. One of the greatest modern theologians, Paul Tillich, has traced more sensitively than anyone else in our time the progress of this tendency toward manipulation as the key to life. He calls it "controlling knowledge," and here is what he sees to be the consequences of it:

Man actually has become what controlling knowledge considers him to be, a thing among things, a cog in the dominating machine of production and consumption, a dehumanized object of tyranny or a standardized object of public communication.[4]

[4] *Systematic Theology,* vol. I (University of Chicago Press, 1951), p. 99. Quoted in "The Ontology of Paul Tillich" by J. H. Randall, Jr., in *The Theology of Paul Tillich,* ed. by C. W. Kegley and R. W. Bretall (New York: Macmillan, 1952), p. 146.

The Christian doctrine of God as the source and meaning of life reinforces the deep repugnance that many people feel at the exaltation of manipulative knowledge as the key to existence. Sir Winston Churchill's reply to a social scientist who was predicting the time when human motivations might be controlled by scientific manipulation was, "I shall be content to be dead when that day arrives." If God is the meaning of existence, then not manipulation but faith is the key to significance in life, and not social engineering but love is the norm of the relationships between man and his fellows. What Tillich calls "receiving knowledge"—which might be translated simply by the word "faith"—assumes that there is a structure and meaning and purpose in life which man does not originate but in which he can participate, which is not dependent upon him but does invite his cooperation and accept his sacrifice and self-offering. Does this not describe more fully the human situation than the new heresy which sees life as wholly at the mercy of human decisions?

We have already hinted at another difficulty which this heresy involves, and that is that although it begins by affirming the autonomy of man it ends in despair about his ability to control his destiny at all. It is a simple fact to which even the briefest study of history introduces us that things very seldom turn out as people expect them to. Nothing is more futile than human prophecy. *The New Yorker* magazine has a regular feature called "The Clouded Crystal Ball" department. It does not lack for material. Sometimes men are confounded by the course of events quite outside their control. Sometimes the unpredictable whims of other men upset their best laid plans. Sometimes they are victims of their own desire to fool themselves or of their own irresolution or lack of perseverance. Whatever the reason, the lesson of history is plain: man has very little power to predict or to determine the course of human events. The future has a disturbing way of surprising and disappointing even the most prescient of us.

It was the recognition of this fact about life that helped to fasten the sense of Fate upon the ancient world into which Christianity was born. The goddess Tyche represented the element of chance or luck, and she was so important in the minds of the ancients that as the elder Pliny says, "Chance herself . . . takes the place of God." [5] Part of the reason for this development was the increasing size and complexity of ancient life. It was a world which in contrast to an earlier time seemed quite unmanageable and utterly indifferent to the decisions and efforts of individual men and women. As we know from the Greek drama, this sense of Fate colored the whole conception of the individual's life, and the Greek tragedy dealt with the theme of the inevitability of calamity despite the most heroic efforts of the characters of the play. This sense of being caught in a fixed and predetermined pattern which one was powerless to affect or modify was, by some of the high-minded Stoics, borne with a certain dignity and tranquility (hence the use of the word "stoic" to mean imperturbability). But among large numbers of people it led to superstitions such as astrology and soothsaying.

It is interesting to speculate on how far this is a description of our own present mood. Much of the so-called apathy that is said by some to have settled upon young people in these days is a result of this sense of the vastness and complexity of social life and the unlikelihood that one may in any important sense direct and modify it. The widespread popularity of astrologers, for example, is a sign that for all the brave summons to men to master fate and direct their destiny there is a general sense that the real arbiter of life is beyond our merely human influences. Is is not strictly speaking heretical, by the way, for Christians to call "good luck" to each other as they part? For the Christian, the issues of life are not in the hands of a blind goddess Tyche but in the hands of a provident and loving Lord of life and history.

Someone has said that in the Old Testament the closer the writers approach to humanism the deeper becomes their sense of despair and pessimism. The book of Ecclesiastes, which has so little place in it for the power and reality of a living and loving Father God, falls back upon a kind of fatalism—"that which hath been is now; and that which is to be hath already been"—and this fatalism

---

[5] Quoted in Rudolf Bultmann, *Primitive Christianity in Its Contemporary Setting,* tr. R. H. Fuller (New York: Thames and Hudson), p. 148.

leads to pessimism and futility—"vanity of vanities, saith the Preacher, all is vanity." The practical effect of the declaration of human autonomy under which so many of our generation have been operating for so long is likely to be the same sort of despair. If man is in charge of things, then all we can rely upon is human wisdom and human fortitude and human goodness—and we are not particularly impressed with the quality and quantity of any of those commodities in these days. Life is so obviously not within man's power to control and determine that only two alternatives present themselves—either one is resigned to the workings of a mysterious Fate or one believes that life is under the ultimate control of a holy and righteous God who can work all things together for good. We shall have more to say in a later chapter about the way this Christian understanding of life and history saves the Christian from the extremes both of optimism and despair. It is sufficient to notice here the deeply unsatisfactory character of naturalistic humanism as basis for any kind of resolute and significant living.

The word "heresy" is normally used to designate a religious opinion that claims to be a legitimate interpretation or understanding of a particular theological tradition. For this reason, naturalistic humanism ought not perhaps to be classified as a Christian heresy at all. It has been described at such length because it is a widely held point of view in intellectual circles, but perhaps it ought to be classified as an alternative religion rather than as a heresy. Of course, there are some who would want to use the designation of "Christian" to include the point of view we have been considering, but probably most naturalistic humanists realize that they are worlds apart from anything that could be called traditional Christianity.

The "Positive Thinking" Heresy

The same conviction, however, that man is at the center of the universe and that his choices and purposes hold the only key to the future appears in a modern movement which eagerly insists that it is an authentic—perhaps the only really authentic—version of the traditional faith of the Christian Church. This might be called the "Positive Thinking" heresy, and it has widespread appeal, attested to by the world-wide fame of some of its best known representatives. In some ways, this heresy is the oldest one of all that we shall be considering, for it is a refined form of primitive magic. Magic is the attempt to master techniques which will harness the superhuman forces of life for man's ambitions. The Positive Thinking heresy offers us such techniques in abundance. Here is the blunt claim which one of the leaders of this movement makes for it in one of his best-selling books: "By using the *techniques* outlined here you can modify or change the circumstances in which you now live, assuming control over them rather than continuing to be directed by them." [6] This is essentially the claim made for primitive magic.[7]

The range of the concern of those who hold the "Positive Thinking" heresy is admittedly much narrower than that of naturalistic humanism. Perhaps more realistically, the "Positive Thinking" heresy makes no particular claim to be able to influence the broad course of human history or to contribute any useful suggestions for the resolution of vexing social problems. The focus is on problems of personal relationships—friendships, family life, one's business or profession. Indeed one reads through the literature of this movement and finds almost no reference to the major social issues that perplex our generation—racial integration, control of nuclear armament, democracy vs. a controlled society, coexistence with Communism, development of international agencies like the United

[6] Norman Vincent Peale, *The Power of Positive Thinking* (Englewood, New Jersey: Prentice-Hall, 1952), p. viii. (Underlining mine.)
[7] An astonishingly magical view of prayer has recently been put forward in a little book called *The Power of God in the Growth of Plants* by Franklin Loehr. The book recounts an experiment whereby two pans of planted seed corn were treated in sharply different ways, one pan being prayed over earnestly while the other was ignored and rejected. The prayed-over corn seedlings grew much more rapidly than the neglected seedlings. Ergo, prayer has been scientifically proven. This identification of Christian prayer with a quasi-physical force not unlike primitive magic suggests the extent to which man-centered religion has spread its heresy among our theologically untrained generation.

Nations, etc. Part of the confidence with which the movement recommends its techniques and insists that there is no problem for
which they do not provide the solution is due to the narrow range
of personal, face-to-face relationships toward which attention is
directed.

The emphasis upon techniques such as the repetition of confident phrases (one follower says, "I believe," to himself three times
every morning upon arising) or the manipulation of certain
mechanical devices (a motorist keeps in the glove compartment a
stack of filing cards with Bible texts written on them and flips them
over as he is driving) gives the impression of a thoroughly depersonalized religion. Very little is said about the sovereign mind and
purpose of God; much is made of the things men can say to themselves and can do to bring about their ambitions and purposes. It
is not accidental that the major images which this literature employs
to speak of the religious life and of God are drawn from the realm
of the impersonal forces of nature. One follower reports: "I go to
church to recharge my batteries." Another man reports the sensation he had in a church service where this heresy was being expounded—"I had a feeling as though I had hold of an electric
wire." We are urged "to tap the reserves of power in the universe"
or "to get in touch with the great force that can be released through
prayer." We said in the last chapter that the images which theology
employs are the only tests by which heresy and orthodoxy can be
defined. The predominant use of impersonal symbols for God is
a serious and dangerous invitation to regard man as the center of
reality and the Divine Reality as an impersonal power, the use and
purpose of which is determined by the man who takes hold of it
and employs it as he thinks best.

The symbolism of orthodox Christian theology has always been
a symbolism derived from personal relationships. When this test
is applied to "Positive Thinking" its heretical character is at once
apparent. Mary Pickford once wrote a book called *Why Not Try
God?* But when one reflects upon it, that language is as shocking
as it would be to ask "Why not try your mother?" One doesn't
"try" or use or employ friends and relatives and those he loves.

The thought of one man manipulating and using another man is deeply distasteful and represents a terrible degradation of human relationships. How much more is this so in the case of God? One dare not approach God as One whom we can make use of, who exists to wait on us and do our bidding. Bishop Fulton J. Sheen once called such a conception of God the picture of "a Cosmic Plumber." The Bible says that God uses us, that we must yield ourselves to his service, that our fulfillment consists in making ourselves available to him for the accomplishment of his purposes. It is impossible to imagine Amos or Isaiah deciding to practice the life of religious faith so that they might live more effectively and successfully. Can anyone think that the first apostles would have described the thing which drew them into his service in terms like this: "Your relations with other people will improve. You will become a more popular, esteemed, and well-liked individual. . . . You may attain a degree of health not hitherto known by you"? To interpret the call of Christianity in this way is to turn the relationship between God and man completely upside down. It is God whose purpose rules the world. It is God who calls on us to become his instruments. By depersonalizing God and making him a force on which we may call for our narrow ambitions is to distort the whole Bible and the whole meaning of the Christian faith.

Inevitably in a pragmatic generation such as ours, someone will reply to all this, "But it works." The testimonials that many "Positive Thinking" movements can produce are overwhelming and impressive. Success, of course, is based on the appeal such a movement makes by reason of the results it has achieved in healing disordered lives, redeeming broken human relationships, and improving the quality of personal life in general. The results are impressive enough so that it appears that this answer has to be taken seriously. Can a movement with these results to its credit really be condemned as heretical?

But this raises a logical problem which is very troublesome. Can success be the only test of truth when mutually contradictory religious movements can all point to some impressive successes? If it is argued that "Positive Thinking" must be valid because it is successful, then one must go on to ask whether the same cannot be said of the Shrine of Lourdes, Mary Baker Eddy, and Oral Roberts. But all of these disagree with each other on fundamental points of theological understanding. Who is right? Obviously the success of the movement which can be seen and measured here and now is not an adequate method of answering that query. Some of the more superficial human problems can be resolved without recourse to the deep truths of Christianity. One does not need to be a Christian to be healed of a broken leg. There is a healing process in nature itself which, aided and assisted by the skill of medical men, which exists in Christian and non-Christian doctors quite indifferently, can restore the patient to strength and wholeness. But for the Christian faith a broken leg is not the ultimate human problem—though, of course, it will seem very real to someone who suffers from it—nor is the ability to walk again the only ideal toward which human nature is striving.

"Positive Thinking" seems to assume that the whole ideal of human life is a kind of harmonious and successful adjustment to people and things as they exist at present. Now it must be admitted that Christianity does not make a virtue out of maladjustment, and that the Bible and Christian history are full of evidence that a certain integration of the self and a certain vitality and effectiveness are often by-products of the Christian experience of acceptance and redemption through Christ. But such experiences are by-products and not conscious goals of Christian striving. "Positive Thinking" may bring about great effectiveness in personal life, but the larger question—which is what one is to be effective *for*—is apparently not answered by this movement at all. Christianity deals with ultimate problems, and in doing so incidentally resolves some minor problems too. "Positive Thinking" fastens upon the minor problems, tempts people to suppose that these are the major problems, and so short-circuits the search for Christian meaning altogether. If "Positive Thinking" pretended to be no more than a technique for mental health and personality adjustment, then it might be welcomed as one welcomes other medical and psychological techniques. When it pretends to be a valid version of the

Christian faith, it has taken on the character of a Christian heresy, and needs to be energetically and carefully sifted and criticized. The injunction in the epistle of St. John to "test the spirits to see whether they are of God," implies that there were in the Church in John's day vigorous and effective movements that in some superficial way "worked," which, nevertheless, John warns his readers are not to be taken as a real part of the Christian life. Short-term success is no way to test Christianity, which by its message of a Crucified Christ proves that the short-range look is often deceptive.

The Heresy of Secularism

Finally, the most subtle and pervasive heresy of all that can be considered under this general heading of man's attempt to make himself the center of life is what is often called "secularism." Someone once called it "the practice of the absence of God." While not denying God's centrality and reality, secularism pays no attention to him and his purposes in the direction of the life of the world. A friend of mine once compared the modern world's attitude toward God to the kind of deference which a parish pays to a rector emeritus. It is pleasant to have the old fellow about, and on ceremonial occasions he graces the head table and there is an opportunity to greet him and say nice things about him. But the effective leadership of the parish is now in new hands, and the new young rector and a vigorous vestry get on with new plans for the parish without consulting the rector emeritus at all. Secularism does not bother denying the reality of God; it is content to ignore him when urgent decisions are being made.

Secularism must be seen against the background of the development of Christian ideas in Western culture, for secularism is a kind of luxury which only a deeply Christianized culture would have dreamt of trying to afford. In a way, secularism ignores God because the kinds of power and conviction which an encounter with him bestows are taken for granted as a natural inheritance of idealism and enthusiasm. Elton Trueblood has made famous the analogy of a cut flower, which continues to bloom gloriously even after it has been severed from its root but which finally and eventually fades and dies and has no power to reproduce itself. Secularism is like that. It had its origins in a set of convictions about what life was like, what its ultimate purpose and final meaning were; and having contented itself with that (which was largely a gift of Christian faith about life), it turned its back on such questions and determined henceforth to deal only with questions which could be accurately and scientifically measured and weighed and "proved."

Viewed historically, secularism was a necessary development of man's mentality in order that he might tackle imaginatively and freely the practical problems of managing and controlling his life. As long as men insisted on discussing only the ultimate explanations of things—which, of course, was the mind and purpose of God—the proximate explanations tended to be left undiscussed and undiscovered. Now there is no essential conflict between the two kinds of questions, but in practice men tend to see them as opposed to one another. An interesting example has been brought to our attention by Mr. T. D. Kendrick in his fascinating study of *The Lisbon Earthquake*. In the wake of this dreadful catastrophe two kinds of explanations were put forward—one we should call scientific and the other religious. Admittedly, the scientific explanations were not very good ones—spontaneous fires exploding combinations of air and water—but the point was that they were put forward as an alternative suggestion to the more popular one advanced by the clergy, namely, that the Lisbon earthquake was a divine punishment upon human sin (and Protestant and Jansenist saw a peculiar appropriateness in Lisbon's being a center of Jesuit influence). Are these two explanations really alternatives? Is it not possible to say both that earthquakes are caused by movements of the earth's crust under pressures which can be measured and tested and also that earthquakes may be intended as a way of sobering men's optimism and facing them up to the fact of their essential weakness and mortality? Both the scientists and the clergy of 1755 were somewhat inaccurate, perhaps, in the way they attempted to "explain" the Lisbon earthquake, but both had a valid purpose in mind—and the purposes were not logically, although perhaps psychologically, inconsistent. Any event may be seen in terms of its immediate or scientific cause, and it may also be seen in terms of its usefulness in the purposes of almighty God for the souls of men. Just as one may "explain" his own birth by the strictly scientific explanations of procreation and obstetrics and at the same time be convinced that he has been brought into the world by God to fulfill a certain purpose and meaning, so any event in the world has two explanations, and in deciding which kind of explanation to concentrate on, man makes an eventful and weighty decision.

Secularism represents a decision to concentrate on the explanations that can be demonstrated, tested, and proved by empirical investigation. This was historically a useful decision. It produced the great flowering of scientific knowledge, the benefits of which we still enjoy. The question is whether such a narrowing of the scope of inquiry is permanently adequate, or even possible for the ranging curiosity of man. There is evidence that in our day in which men are learning about *how* things operate so that they know how to do almost anything, there is a desperate uncertainty about *why* things happen and whether anything is worth doing at all. The joyful freedom with which the men of the Renaissance broke out into a search for the natural causes of things has given way to a weariness and a malaise of spirit which is the chief burden of much modern literature and modern art.

The answer of Christian orthodoxy to secularism is not to deny the usefulness of any of its questions or conclusions nor, as we shall see in a moment, to endeavor to reassert ecclesiastical domination over man's cultural life. Christian orthodoxy is only concerned that the questions of meaning and purpose, and the answers to those questions which are found in the Christian revelation of the being and purpose of God, shall continue to form the background for the inquiries with which secular thought has so energetically concerned itself. The motto of Christian orthodoxy is:

"All this and heaven too." Christianity would welcome every discovery and technique which may help make this life more comfortable, more convenient, and more enjoyable. But it would insist that this life can only be understood in the light of the final purpose for which human nature was created, namely, to express qualities of faith, freedom, responsibility, and love which are seen in their fullness in the life and death of Jesus Christ. The heresy of secularism, like most other heresies we shall be considering, consists in its one-sidedness and narrowness. It is correct in most of what it affirms; it is in error in most of what it denies. One of the curious superstitions of modern thought is that Christian orthodoxy is narrowing and restricting in its outlook and influence. Certainly in contrast with modern secularism, the precise opposite is the truth. Christianity makes room for every positive expression of humanism, but much dogmatic secularism would deny the legitimacy or relevance of man's religious life.

The Anti-Secularist Heresy

But if secularism is a heresy, there is an opposite one into which some apologists for the Christian faith tend to fall and that is to turn to the Church for an answer and to impose some sort of ecclesiastical control once again over the cultural and scientific life of mankind. This was one of the issues at the time of the Reformation. With the rallying cry, "Let the Church be the Church," the Reformers—at least Lutherans and Anglicans—agreed that the Church's task was essentially a religious one, preaching the Gospel and administering the sacraments, and that those who managed the secular affairs of mankind were independently responsible to God but not to the Church. The late Archbishop Temple described the situation in a way that will be familiar to all Englishmen. "It is the duty of Westminster (i.e., the government) to obey God, and it is the duty of Lambeth (i.e., the Church) to remind Westminster of this fact. But it is not the duty of Westminster to obey Lambeth, and Lambeth would be guilty of usurpation of authority if it demanded such obedience." [8] Dr. Temple is in a distinguished Anglican tradition in discriminating in this way as to the role of the Church in man's social life, for it was the great sixteenth-century Anglican, Richard Hooker, who suggested in his *Laws of Ecclesiastical Polity* that man's reason had an autonomy and a capacity of its own to manage many of the affairs of life and that only in matters having to do with his salvation was man dependent upon the Bible as the source of truth.

One area where this antisecularist heresy is vigorous today is in the field of education. The answer can be bluntly stated this way: education is not the primary business of the Church, it is the business of educators. One hears a great deal of bewailing of secularism in education, and it is clear enough to anyone who is familiar with education, especially with higher education, that the prevailing point of view is usually a genial, urbane, sophisticated kind of humanism in which very little attempt is made to raise questions of man's destiny and purpose and significance. There are exceptions to this over-all picture, but it is probably still a fairly accurate description of the modern college campus. In view of this, there is often heard a rallying cry to crusade for more church colleges. But a close look at the church colleges which we already support raises a question as to how much practical difference in prevailing viewpoint, especially in the classroom, can be found to mark the church college off from the general average of the small liberal arts colleges which have no official church connection. Wherever the Church has inherited a responsibility for education, by all means let it exercise that responsibility to the best of its ability. It does not, however, seem to be strategic at the moment to multiply ecclesiastical controls over education until we are sure that the Church has done her utmost to lead individual Christian teachers into the kind of deep understanding of Christian truth which can just as effectively be expressed in a secular college as in one that carries the official name and sponsorship of the Church.

[8] William Temple, "Christian Faith and the Common Life" in *Christian Faith and the Common Life* (New York: Willett & Clark Co., 1938), p. 56.

To tack the Church's name over an educational institution and to have more bishops on the board of directors does nothing automatically to insure that Christian insight will permeate the teaching or illuminate the minds of the students. Contrariwise, if a Christian teacher is both a skillful teacher and a believing Christian, there is no way he or she can be stopped from leading students into Christian insights, at least not in most of the secular colleges as they are presently organized. The main question any college has to face is that of the quality of its teachers and of the range and depth of their sensitivity, concern, and curiosity. The ideal of the *Christian* teacher includes a deep understanding of the Christian faith and its relationship to the whole of man's life. Unfortunately the number of such teachers is small, and this is the real problem to which the Church ought to turn its attention rather than toward the extension of ecclesiastical controls.

The heresy of secularism is best confronted not by ecclesiastical imperialism but by theological orthodoxy. That man has wide areas of freedom and responsibility is part of the biblical doctrine of his creation in the image of God. But the myth of the Garden of Eden says that this freedom and responsibility are both the source of splendid insight and imaginative aspiration and also the source of overweening pride and limitless ambition. Everything man touches will be corrupted by his tendency to make himself the center of existence. The solution to this problem does not lie in ecclesiastical imperialism, for man has touched the Church, too, and its history is proof that it is not immune from these tendencies to self-aggrandizement and overweening pride. The solution lies in the preaching of the doctrine of human sin and that man lives by faith in God's forgiveness of that sin. As we shall see, these doctrines also have fallen victim to heretical tendencies in modern thought, and they deserve a chapter to themselves. Meanwhile, we may formulate orthodoxy's answer to this heresy that man is the center of the universe in this way: man is a creature of God and to him he owes his existence, his reason, his freedom, and all that he has and is, but God made man for freedom and responsibility; and as a father seeks to draw his son into a mature relationship, not of slavish obedience but of a glad sharing of insight and purpose, so God calls us into a service in which we find our destiny in the glorious liberty of the sons of God. We are neither so autonomous as our modern heresy assumes, nor are we such puppets as authoritarian ecclesiasticism assumes. Orthodoxy confers on us a status as sons of God, and that phrase exactly describes both the fullness of our freedom and the depth of our dependence.

CHAPTER THREE

The Personal God

*I*s God a "He" or an "It"? That question—or a less crude and brutal form of the same sort of inquiry—lies at the center of much contemporary thinking about religion. There is a widespread and frequently expressed preference for declining to speak of God in personal terms, and choosing rather to speak of a Divine Power or a Process of Value Realization or to use other impersonal language. The reasons for this preference are not altogether clear. It may be due in part to the problem of imaginative conception of God in view of the vast and enormous development of scientific knowledge about the universe. The hero of Robert Briffault's novel *Europa* is greatly moved by the Michelangelo murals of the Creation in the Sistine Chapel of the Vatican, but one night a friend lets him peer through a telescope at the great Andromeda nebula, spinning away as a whole universe of energy, unimaginable distances away. After that glimpse into the vastness of interstellar space, Michelangelo's picture of an old man stretching out his hand to call the worlds into being no longer seems to the young man a compelling or adequate picture of God. That may be the problem with us. Our conception of personality—a self-conscious unity of will and thought and feeling—seems out of place in a vast universe, the extent of whose energies and processes would challenge the power of any mind of which we know anything to control and direct.

The Concept of God

Sometimes the reason given is simply human modesty. Isn't it presumptuous, we are asked, to project the image of man upon the supreme source and ultimate reality behind all things? One of the signs of childishness and superstition is to personalize the forces of nature. So a child kicks at a stone over which he has stumbled and castigates it as if it were a person who had deliberately sought to harm him. Perhaps this sort of personification is useful at a primitive level of thought. Perhaps it is desirable, for example, to personify the spirit of kindliness and good will at Christmas time by the figure of a jolly little man in a fur-trimmed red suit. But some time or other children learn that "there is no Santa Claus" except as he is the personification of certain qualities of the human spirit which reach their height at Christmas time. So in the maturity of the human race the personality of God must be abandoned. The figure of a personal God points to an important truth about life—it has a drive and a direction to it—but we no longer take the figure literally any more than we believe in a Santa Claus who lives at the North Pole and drives a sleigh drawn by reindeer.

As we saw in the first chapter, there is a great sympathy among traditional orthodox theologians with the hesitation to speak too precisely and too anthropomorphically (that is, in personal or human language) about God. For those who want to stress the transcendence of God over all human language about him, there is substantial support from the Bible itself. God is often described in the Bible by means of the forces of nature—thunder, lightning, blinding light, smoke, the power of an earthquake. "The whole earth

is full of his glory" is a way of saying that hints of his power are
to be found in all the aspects of the created order—in the majestic
wheeling of the Andromeda nebula and in the dynamics of atomic
structures. But the Bible at the very moment it is speaking in such
sublime and awesome language adds always the element of personal challenge and confrontation. As Isaiah saw the vision of God
in the Temple, "high and lifted up . . . the house was filled with
smoke . . . the posts of the door were moved at the voice of him
that cried," he also heard a voice out of that ineffable glory which
spoke directly to him, "Whom shall we send and who will go for
us?" That is the insistent message of the Bible—the God of glory
and majesty and power is also the God who speaks to you and
to me, who calls and claims and summons us, who speaks to us
and—most unbelievable of all—heeds our answer.

The problem of God's power and how it can be made to fit
the idea of God as a Personal Being who seeks personal relationships with men has troubled modern thought a very great deal.
Erich Fromm and Joshua L. Liebman, among others, have argued
that a God of absolute power is a Being with whom no one could
ever come into any satisfactory personal relationship at all—except
perhaps the relationship of infinite resentment. In international
politics, to take one example, it is obvious that a nation of great
power, no matter how tactfully and delicately it seeks to behave
itself, encounters resentment from weaker nations who cannot help
but feel threatened by the menace of omnipotence. Is this not inevitably the case with man's relationship to an omnipotent God?
Is it not natural that as believers in democracy, modern men must
resist what appears to be the final tyranny of all, the tyranny of
an all-powerful God?

The Concept of a "Limited" God

To meet this difficulty some modern theologians (one
or two professional ones but an even larger number of that amateur
kind who must perforce perform theologically every Sunday in their

pulpits) have more or less boldly asserted their belief in a limited and finite God who cannot do whatever he wants to do. One representative of this tendency wrote some years ago: "The advance in modern thought has compelled us to modify our faith either in God's character or in his omnipotence. . . . On our view, God is perfect in will, but not in achievement." [1] This view is echoed, perhaps largely unconsciously, in many American pulpits. A friend of mine has characterized most preaching which he hears as consisting of "if-only" sermons: "If only people would obey the Sermon on the Mount, the world would be ever so much better." The image of God that such sermons project is of a Divine floor-pacer, wringing his hands over the mess men are getting into and wishing desperately he could think of something to do about it. How often one hears in sermons phrases like this: "God is trying to do so and so"; "God hopes we will hear and obey him." Some of this language is inevitable as the language of analogy, but we ought to be quite sure we see how very misleading it can be. God isn't really "trying" to do anything; he is doing it. God doesn't "hope" for anything; he is quite aware that his will is done perfectly both in earth and in heaven. The danger of talking about a limited God who is trying things out and hoping things will work out well is that one can put no confidence or trust in such a God. For if a limited and finite God is really our image of the Divine then he may very well fail. Perhaps our experience with democracy has misled us into thinking that God is not so much the eternal King of creation as just a candidate seeking that office (and the preachers are his precinct workers, out drumming up votes). But what if he isn't elected?

Orthodoxy's answer to this heresy has always been the assertion that God can do anything he wants, but what he wants is to create free beings able to respond to him wholeheartedly and trustingly. Omnipotence is not the ability to do anything; it is the ability to achieve one's purpose. God is not able to make two and two equal five, but that is no real limitation on him, because he

[1] E. S. Brightman, *The Problem of God* (New York: Abingdon, 1930), p. 137.

doesn't want to! Omnipotence as men usually understand it is the ability to impose one's will upon another. The omnipotence of God is the ability to win men's loyalty and trust and faith, to capture their hearts as a lover captures the heart of his beloved. Omnipotence is not the opposite of freedom but rather, in a special sense, the necessary condition of freedom.[2] If one visits a preparatory school and sees everything rigidly controlled by rules and regulations, one can guess that the headmaster is not really in very complete control of the situation in that school. The mark of real competence and omnipotence is a school where rules and regulations are at a minimum and where there is genuine freedom guaranteed by the sense that the headmaster is in complete control of the situation at a deeper and far more important level than mere obedience to rules. God's omnipotence is proved by the freedom with which he allows man to run the world as he wants. If he were interfering all the time, shrilly insisting that men hew to the line and seizing them by the scruff of the neck if they did not, one would conclude that he was a very nervous and uncertain Deity, indeed. God's omnipotence lies in his capacity to make all things work together for good, finally and ultimately. Perhaps the most powerful evidence for this is the story of the Cross and the Resurrection of Jesus Christ.

Alternative to a Personal God

The man who hesitates to speak, as the Bible speaks, of God as personal must be asked to consider the implications of the alternative that is possible. Not to speak of God as personal leaves only one alternative—to speak of God as impersonal. The limitations of our language are such that if we refuse to use personal words about God, we must employ subpersonal words. A favorite word that some people employ who don't like to speak of God as personal is the word "force." The word "force" is borrowed from

[2] I owe this illustration which follows to a lecture by the Reverend E. L. Mascall in a course at Christ Church, Oxford.

physics. It denotes something like electricity which is purposeless and mindless, can harm as well as help, runs about automatically, given certain physical conditions. To speak of God as a force, as we have already seen, ministers to the illusion that man is in charge and that God is a power which man ought properly to gain control over and bend to his purposes. There may be dangers in speaking of God as "He"; they are far less insidious and subversive of the Christian experience than the dangers of speaking of God as "It."

What is at stake in using personal language about God is whether there is any meaning or purpose in reality, for if God is not at least a person in the sense that he conceives plans and realizes purposes—and nothing subhuman has that power—then the conclusion is that there is no purpose in life at all. Purpose is something which mind creates. If there is no ultimate mind behind existence, then there is no fundamental purpose in it, and the heresy of man at the center of things is inevitable. The persistence of man's questions about "why" and his refusal to find a satisfactory answer only in terms of "how" is evidence that man naturally assumes some underlying and all-pervading purpose in life. If that assumption is valid, then there is a mind behind things that exist, and that is the justification for speaking of God as personal. Orthodox theology is aware of the dangers of this bold step and would say that only by way of analogy can such language be anything but seriously misleading; but sensing the alternatives, orthodoxy believes there can be no question of the choice. God is at least as personal as we are—not less so—and that means that he conceives purposes and brings them to fulfillment.

Another conclusion follows from the assertion that God is personal. That is, that the disclosure of his purpose must be by his own act and his own word. If our image of man's relationship to God is an image of personal relationships, then there must be such a thing as revelation, the opening up the heart and mind of God to man. In personal relationships, one man cannot raid the privacy of the heart and mind of the other. It is the privilege of men to withhold the secrets of the self from others. Self-disclosure is a selective and, at least in large measure, a free decision. Of course, we can find out something about another person without his active cooperation. We can photograph and weigh and measure him, fluoroscope and x-ray him, and compile a very substantial amount of information about him. But when a man has all this information about another man piled up on his desk, we should agree that in an important sense he still knows nothing about the other man. We mean that he knows nothing about what he is up to, what "makes him tick," what he desires and loves and seeks above everything else.

The Heresy of Deism

One of the heresies which has had wide currency among modern men is the heresy which says that all we know about God is what we can find out about him by observing what might be called his outward actions. This heresy, which had the name of Deism in the eighteenth century, says that what can be known about God is a matter of human investigation and observation and that God's active, personal cooperation in disclosing his mind and heart and purpose is neither necessary nor really believable. In the eighteenth century it was assumed that what men discovered about God all fitted together rather neatly and disclosed him to be a God of architectural and engineering tastes, whose main passion was regularity and consistency. More perceptive studies of religion as a human phenomenon lead modern scholars to question this universal pattern, but the main position has nevertheless continued to be held in a somewhat new form. Now it is fashionable to say that all men have had some insights into God's behavior on the basis of their own experience, and if these insights do not at the moment shape up into any very consistent pattern, then we must be content to say that each approach has its own validity and some day the essential pattern will be made clear. The popular analogy of men approaching the summit of a mountain by separate paths has become threadbare by repetition, but it suggests the point of view of this heresy.

It is heretical chiefly because it rules out, in the case of God, one of the most characteristic aspects of the life of the personal self, and that is disclosure and communication. That God remains aloof and uncommunicative, allowing himself to be poked at and probed and investigated but never taking the initiative and opening up in any revealing and communicative way, is a very unsatisfactory image of personal existence. Such a human being is rightly thought to be seriously and pathetically psychotic. Isn't Deism, in its image of an uncommunicative and withdrawn God, open to the charge of imagining God as a person fit only for radical psychoanalysis? Such a shut-up and withdrawn God could certainly never produce the faith and devotion and love which have been conspicuous marks of the Christian religious attitude and experience. However dangerous such language is, Christians must always say that God is One who speaks and acts, who discloses himself in decisive action and illuminating word, who in the beginning was a Word, seeking to express and communicate the divine purpose to men. We are not left to speculate on the purpose of God, especially his purpose for us and our destiny. Such speculation can produce only confusion, for the experiences of life as a whole are, on the surface at least, contradictory and ambiguous. It is no wonder that the great religions of the world differ in many important ways, for life is such a rich and variegated tapestry that different people will see it in different lights. Christianity rests upon a fundamental assumption—that God has disclosed enough of his mind and purpose in special moments, events, and persons so that we are led to trust him for life and death and find in him the meaning of our existence. "Is there a God?" was the first question that an American professor of theology in Japan used to ask his students, but he immediately followed it with an equally important one, "Does he *do* anything?" Christianity says that he does something all-important for man's life: he reveals and discloses his heart and his mind and his purpose in such a way that we can respond in devotion and gratitude.

The Heresy of Universalism

The selection of special events and persons as the medium for this revelation has seemed to the modern mind to be essentially arbitrary and whimsical. Is it intellectually respectable to believe that God would choose a nation of people like the ancient Hebrews out of all the other peoples of the earth and through their history reveal such all-important realities as his plan and purpose for all people everywhere? Surely anything as important and world-shaking ought to be available for men generally and not reserved as the special prerogative of a single nation. As we have learned more about other great world religions—and especially come to see them in a more favorable light as a result of acquaintance with higher aspects of their teaching and practice— there has been almost inevitably a tendency to raise questions about the uniqueness of the Bible, of the revelation to Israel, and of the Incarnation of God in the man Jesus. All of this claim to special and unique revelation seems to the modern mind to be part of what has been called "the scandal of particularity"—the idea that in this historic moment or movement rather than in any other God has drawn aside in an all-important and decisive way the veil of mystery which hides his Being and purpose. What might be called the heresy of universalism would hold that God is not selective but generalized and universal in his revelation. He is to be found at all times and in all places, always disclosing himself to any devout man or woman who seeks him, disclosing his purpose in the great universal experience of natural life rather than in the special history of this particular country or era.

Like most heresies, this one has hold of a part of the truth. There is a universal religious longing and there is an impressive amount of agreement among the great world religions. Indeed Christianity itself has held, as early as the New Testament, that God has not left himself without witness among any people and that Christ is the true Light which lightens every man who comes into the world. There is a genuine universalism about Christianity. It believes that it is meant for all people everywhere, that it meets needs and answers questions which men have been asking themselves always, often led to these questions by the very insights which their own religions have given them. What is at stake, however, is whether God takes history and individuality seriously. Are the particular and unique experiences of historical life of any significance at all for the discovery of truth? Must all truth be equally available to everyone at once, public property for all who can qualify by using minimum rationality and logic? Is there not another kind of truth, a kind which dawns upon one man only, a man unique because of the combination of background and temperament and genius which has formed him? God takes history and individuality seriously, and so it is quite conceivable that he can choose, for example, Amos, the sheepherder of Tekoa, as the one to whom he will reveal something about the sovereignty of the divine justice which had occurred to no one else in such sharp and compelling terms. Even wise human parents take into account the responsiveness and sensitivity of their children in deciding to what sorts of experience they will introduce them and when. So God elects some individuals—and, in the case of Israel, a whole nation—to be the vehicle of truth about himself and his purpose for the sake of the whole world.

One of the criticisms that the universalist heresy makes about the orthodox view of special revelation is that it encourages theological snobbery, the kind of snobbery that is reflected in a well-known missionary hymn: "Can we whose souls are lighted by wisdom from on high; Can we to men benighted the lamp of life deny?" But this criticism, justified as it may be by hymns like that, misses the point of God's election. God's choice is prompted by only one thing—the willingness and capacity of the person or nation chosen to tell the story of God's dealings with them. The surprising thing about Israel is the faithful, humble, and realistic way it describes its own failings, stupidities, inadequacies, and faults, despite God's providence and mercy. That would appear to be why God chose this otherwise fairly unremarkable people.

They could be depended on to tell a story—straight and frank—though it condemned them and showed them up as it was being told. One might say the same thing for the early Christian disciples, who, as it has often been remarked, show up in the Gospels as extraordinarily clumsy, uncomprehending, and undependable. Yet it was the disciples themselves who told the stories by which we condemn them. This preoccupation with God which permits a man to be utterly realistic about himself and so lets God's glory shine through is the single quality which determines God's election, although to put it completely accurately, that quality itself is God's gift and inspiration.

The ravages of the universalist heresy are most clearly seen in the loss in the contemporary Church of her sense of mission. One does not need to rehearse here the dreary evidence for this loss. Dwindling budgets, shrinking numbers of candidates for missionary undertaking, pitifully unimaginative strategies—all are signs that the modern Church is not quite sure what responsibility it has for those who are not already within its walls. This uncertainty is especially felt with respect to places abroad where great world religions are exhibiting impressive signs of revival and reform. Why, it is argued, should we attempt to impose our religion on a people who have had a religion of their own for thousands of years? There is only one answer to that. Christianity is not "our religion" but a story in which God has disclosed in a determinative and crucial way his loving purpose for all human life. Christianity is not native to America, of course, nor to England or western Europe. Its origins were in the Middle East, and it might be observed that it was strongly represented both in India and China hundreds of years before America was ever discovered by white men. If the Christian story had really been understood and the fullness of its meaning experienced, there would be no such sophisticated quibbling about its relevance or appropriateness. No poet, passionately convinced of the truth and beauty that can be evoked by his poetry, hesitates to have it published or read on the grounds that "people already have their own poetry and they seem contented with it." The power of what he has been permitted to see and express so possesses him that he must share and communicate it with as many other people as possible. Poetic truth may very well be something which has found a unique expression in one man's work, and he should feel obliged to share it as widely as possible. The analogy is inadequate, but it suggests the kind of passionate responsibility that has always possessed the Christian Church at its best. The surest sign that our modern thinking about God and his revelation has been dangerously infected by heresy is the weakened conviction that we have anything unique and all-important to tell to the world.

Divine Revelation

In all that we have been saying about revelation it should have been clear that we have not been talking about anything less than the revelation of the life and heart of God himself. This revelation is not one of information but of personal intention and purpose. The image that some people have of revelation is of God imparting in some mechanical way instructions or propositions which it is our duty to obey and accept as a sign of our loyalty to him. The motion picture *The Ten Commandments* ministered to this illusion by depicting the giving of the Commandments on Mount Sinai as a kind of invisible trip-hammer chiseling out the words on stone tablets. Such a picture is heretical, because it pictures both the human and the divine roles in the revelation experience in a false way. God does not reveal himself as a kind of celestial tombstone carver, nor is man's role that of a stunned and passive onlooker. The picture of the prophet Hosea, where God is depicted as the loving husband of a notoriously unfaithful wife, is far truer to the insight which the New Testament offers us as to what revelation means. Revelation means the involvement of God in human history, entering into it in ways we shall have occasion to think about in a later chapter, finally in the Incarnation bearing in a personal way all the pain and ugliness and sin of it. And this personal disclosure of God's own heart and purpose must be received—not just by passive and awe-struck amazement—but by answering trust and loyalty and appropriation through faith. We cannot describe even remotely what happened on Mount Sinai—and one of the drawbacks to religious motion pictures is that they feel impelled to supply what the Bible itself has the taste and sensitivity to keep veiled in reticence and mystery—but whatever happened was a highly personal encounter and relationship. A winning and persuasive and gripping word of God found response in the mind and heart of Moses. That is the way it must have been, because revelation is a self-disclosure of One who is personal.

By this test, one must judge whatever claims are made concerning authentic revelation of the Divine. A case in point is the proclamation in 1954 of the dogma of the Assumption of the Blessed Virgin Mary. The question that must be asked about this dogma is how it can be said to be in any way a disclosure of the heart and purpose of God. To many students of theology, the dogma appears to be mainly a statement about the whereabouts of the body of the Lord's mother. How does that information, supposing it to be true, increase my trust or deepen my commitment to God? Indeed what does it really mean to have faith in such a proposition—unless faith means nothing more than credulity? The Assumption of the Virgin Mary bodily into heaven may be legitimate as a subject of reverent speculation by devout people who in their love of Christ would seek to honor his mother. There is no harm in this, though our Lord warns us that such adulation ought not to deflect us from the more essential responsibility of hearing the word of God and keeping it (cf. Luke 11: 28). But to elevate such speculations to the status of divine revelation discloses a seriously heretical understanding of what revelation is and of the meaning of the life of faith.

The practical test of revelation, then, is the extent to which it builds up faith and deepens trust and quickens response and obedience. In the welter of religious opinion which is all around us today—and it would appear that no religious theory is so absurd that money cannot be found for its propagation nor adherents

found to celebrate it—the question must always be: what consequences does the acceptance of this supposed revelation have for
my life of faith and obedience? Much of such opinion is utterly
irrelevant for the living of a Christian life. If it is, then it is not
divine revelation, because God is not running a celestial Ency-
clopaedia Britannica. He is seeking and winning and saving the
souls of men, and his disclosure of himself is for that purpose and
to that end only.

Revelation and Mystery

If revelation is a personal relationship, then there
must be large areas of mystery surrounding it, for mystery is a
concomitant of relationships between free persons. No man ever
fully understands another. Husband and wife, having lived together for forty years, are still something of a puzzle to one another. "What in the world made her do that?" the husband asks,
though he has shared much of her life, her dreams, her aspira-
tions. This continuing mystery is a mark of freedom. It means that
completely confident prediction about human behavior is always
impossible, and that human relationships proceed on faith, based
at the most upon significant clues and revealing moments. If this
is so between human beings, how much more true it is between
man and God, the Eternal and Absolute Person. "Thou art a
God that hidest thyself" is simply another way of saying that God
is personal, for it is in the nature of a person to remain in many
ways incomprehensible to another person.

This fact of the ultimate mystery of God's Being establishes
a certain tentativeness about dogmatic formulations of orthodoxy.
They do not, as we have already seen, provide blueprints about
the Being and activity of God. In many ways the few simple
affirmations of orthodoxy make the areas of mystery seem that
much more puzzling. If we say as a dogma that God was in Christ,
a problem like the problem of evil becomes even more difficult and
bewildering. The orthodox believer is not fearfully clutching on

to his supply of dogmas, anxious lest any be snatched away from
him by the course of events or the irrefutable logic of some new
argument. Since the ultimate ground of reality is personal, we
must expect surprises. Indeed it might be argued that one of the
proofs that there is a personal reality behind events is that the
events keep surprising us by the way they turn up and turn out.
The orthodox Christian, confident that life is fundamentally an
encounter with a personal God, is of all men the most flexible,
the most resilient, least likely to be overwhelmed in despair or
reduced to panic when favorite doctrines and ideas must be discarded or radically revised.

The Doctrine of the Holy Trinity

Before we take leave of the idea of a God who is
personal and of some of the currents in modern thinking which
undermine this Christian understanding of him and his relationship to us, we must consider the greatest orthodox dogma of all,
the doctrine of the Holy Trinity. We shall postpone for a later
chapter a consideration of the sources of the doctrine of the Trinity
in the conviction about the divine status of Jesus Christ, although
that is doubtless the most important thing about the Trinity. Here
we shall limit our attention to the ways in which Christians ought
to understand the Trinity as a way of expressing the idea of a
personal God. What one author calls "the mature and final expression" of the doctrine of the Trinity in western Christianity,
namely, the work of St. Augustine, boldly chose to understand this
central dogma in the light of an analogy with the structure of the
human soul. That is to say, personal existence implies a kind of
trinitarian pattern. If one considers and reflects on what is involved in being a person, he will come as close as human thought
can come to grasping the meaning of the doctrine of God as
Trinity.

St. Augustine chose to think about this whole matter primarily
in terms of what he considered to be man's most characteristic

activity, namely, the activity of thought. The most startling thing about our thinking is this: we can think about ourselves. I can set up in my mind an image of myself. I can criticize myself, praise myself, suggest improvements in my behavior, resolve to strengthen certain aspects of my life. All of us have experiences like this all the time in which we exist in a kind of a twofold way. I think, and I am the object of my own thinking. But one can identify a third aspect of the thinking self, that is the effort of the self to bring these other two selves closer together. I seek to draw myself as I am closer to the sort of person I judge I ought to be. In a sense there are three "I's" operating in this process. I reflect, I am reflected upon, and I seek to make the image and the reality coincide more closely. Now, obviously, this human experience is only a very inadequate—and in one aspect quite misleading—analogy of the Divine Reality. The most apparent flaw is that man is a divided and dissatisfied person, and God is a fully unified and realized person. In God the "I" that is and the "I" that I want to be are one and the same. So St. Augustine describes the third "I" in the case of God not as that which strives to unite the image and the reality, but as that which delights in the perfect coincidence of the image and the reality.

A major objection to St. Augustine's analogy is that it is too self-centered. Many would prefer to find the analogy of the Trinity in the human person as a revealing and communicating self rather than as a thinking self. We have already said that in revelation there is a gap of mystery between the one who is known and the one who exists in himself.[3] I make myself known to another person in ways that are appropriate to him. I meet his interests as I know them. I try to "speak his language." But by this very process I do not quite express myself as I fully am. I must render myself in a way that makes contact with him, but to do that I

---

[3] I owe most of this paragraph which follows to an illuminating discussion of this topic in W. Norman Pittenger's *The Word Incarnate* (New York: Harper and Bros., 1959), p. 226. Behind my appreciation of Pittenger's remarks lies a prior debt to Claude Welch's *In This Name* (New York: Chas. Scribner's Sons, 1952), a fuller treatment of the recent discussions of the Trinity.

must in some ways misrepresent myself to him. In the case of God's revealing himself to man this is an even more serious problem. As we read in the book of Exodus, when Moses besought God, "Shew me thy glory," God's answer must be, "Thou canst not see my face, for there shall no man see me and live." The full reality of God is too staggering and stunning a vision. Man's freedom and responsibility would shrivel and die before such power and glory. So God must transform himself and come within the limits of our powers of conception. Martin Buber has said that an anthropomorphic God is not a consequence of human presumption but of divine condescension. It is God who decides to be anthropomorphic for our sakes. He speaks to us—a staggering idea if we have any picture at all of God's nature as absolute and transcendent reality. He becomes man—an even more staggering idea which prompts Catholic ceremonial to direct a profound bow or a genuflection as these words are repeated in the Nicene Creed. One final fact emerges from our reflection on the process of divine revelation, and that is that God is not content to accommodate himself to our capacities. He also creates in our hearts and minds the capacity to receive, to accept the disclosure, to be able to perceive the Divine Reality in the deceptively simple form. God is the One who eternally is; he is the One who takes a human form and addresses and confronts us; he is the One who works in our hearts to enable us to receive and appropriate more and more the meaning of his self-disclosure.

The Meaning of "Person"

One of the most widespread modern heresies is simply the neglect of this doctrine of the Trinity rather than any particular distorted version of it. Part of the reason for this neglect is the rather unfortunate language—from the point of view of modern terminology—in which the doctrine is expressed. To say that there is One God in Three Persons is misleading to many people, who at once leap to the conclusion that Christianity imagines three distinct personalities joined together in a sort of heavenly executive committee meeting all the time.[4] "Persons" is probably a poor word to use for modern readers or listeners because it has come to mean an individual personality, an intensely self-conscious center of will and purpose and desire. If there are three such personalities in the Godhead, then Christianity has apparently abandoned the faith in One God and gone in for tritheism. But in the sense of personality, there is only one Person, that is God. It is his mind, his purpose, his desire that we come to know and trust. Our praises are addressed to him—not to "them." [5] St. Augustine was uneasy about using the term "Persons," and his uneasiness is shared by many modern theologians. What the doctrine tries to say is that within the single mind and heart and will of God there are three roles, three ways by which God exists as God (a phrase that Professor Welch prefers), three relationships. Again one may have recourse to an analogy of human relationship and revelation. A man discloses different aspects of himself to different persons in different situations. He is the father of his family, and his family know him in a certain role and for a certain purpose. He is a businessman, and his customers and business colleagues know him also in a certain role and for a certain purpose. He is, let us say, a member of the School Board of his community, and the personnel of the school system and the citizens of the community know him in a different role and for a different purpose. Unfortunately a single man cannot fulfill his responsibilities in all three roles and relationships simultaneously and on a full time basis, and here the analogy breaks down. But God is eternally three in his personal existence and as he reveals and discloses himself to us. He is working full-time, so to speak,

[4] There is a school of thought which seems to hold very much this sort of a view, though with enough qualifications so that they are probably within the pale of orthodoxy. This group of theologians hold to what is called "the Social Doctrine of the Trinity." An example is Leonard Hodgson's *The Doctrine of the Trinity* (New York: Scribner's, 1944).
[5] It is interesting to notice that the *Gloria* in the Prayer Book version of *Benedicite Omnia Opera* reads: "Let us bless the Father and the Son and the Holy Ghost: praise *him* and magnify *him forever*. (Italics mine.)

in his threefold activity, putting all the divine energy into the expression of his mind and will and purpose as Father, Son, and Holy Spirit. A man is three—or more—persons, but only successively and temporarily. God is three Persons eternally and everlastingly and fully, and in each Person his whole mind and intention is perfectly and completely fulfilled.

The Consequences of Doctrinal Neglect

Widespread modern failure to grasp and understand this doctrine has led to distressing theological confusion. Sometimes the failure is conscious and deliberate. An announcement in a southern California newspaper declared that the next Sunday was Trinity Sunday, "a day celebrating a doctrine which is notoriously difficult to understand. The rector will preach an appropriate sermon." One fears that he did exactly that! But to neglect the doctrine of the Trinity results in a one-sided experience of Christianity. Professor H. Richard Niebuhr has described the forms these distortions take.[6] There is the "religion of the Father," which is the worship of the Creator of nature. There is the "religion of the Son, which is the worship of God in Jesus Christ," illustrated by some of our more popular hymns and, one is afraid, some of our more popular sermons. "O, Master, let me walk with thee" never lifts its eyes beyond the level of what St. Paul would have described as "knowing Jesus Christ after the flesh." In contrast, the Church's Christmas hymns strike a sensitive balance between "What child is this who, laid to rest, on Mary's lap is sleeping" and "Veiled in flesh the Godhead see, Hail the incarnate deity." Thirdly there is the religion of the Spirit, stressing the inner light which each man receives and which gives personal direction and meaning to his life. Taken together these experiences verify and illustrate the meaning of the doctrine of the Trinity; separated

[6] Cf. "The Doctrine of the Trinity and the Unity of the Church" in *Theology Today*, October, 1946, III, 3, pp. 371-384, quoted in Claude Welch, *op. cit.*, pp. 227-228.

from each other, each can become a distortion of the full picture
of what Christianity believes God is and is doing.

An illustration of the havoc wrought by the neglect of the doctrine of the Trinity is the misunderstanding of the doctrine of the
Atonement which follows from it. Lin Yu Tang in a book written
many years ago (I believe he has since become a Presbyterian
and, one hopes, a sound Trinitarian believer) described his understanding of the Atonement like this: "When [Adam's] posterity
murdered God's only Son, God was so delighted that He forgave
them all." [7] If the doctrine of the Trinity is rightly understood,
there can be no such separation between God the Father and God
the Son. They are not distinct personalities, so that one can rejoice in the suffering of the other. "God was *in* Christ," and if
that is so then there is no possible distinction between the heart
and mind of the Father and the heart and mind of the Son. Christianity precisely rejects the notion that a loving Jesus-god appeased
the wrath of a fierce Father-god. We shall have more to say in a
later chapter about the Atonement, but it can never be understood
at all unless one first understands what the Church is trying to
say in the doctrine of the Trinity.

We have begun to see already how interwoven theological
doctrines are. Someone has coined the phrase "the seamless robe
of Christian theology" to epitomize this fact that all doctrines are
interdependent with all others. But the doctrine of God is surely
fundamental, and heresy here is obviously fatal for the whole enterprise of Christian thought and Christian life. Underlying much
of the theological confusion in the minds of many devout Christian people is the failure to hold fast to the very simple but profound idea that although God is unlike anything else we know,
he is most like the best Person one can ever know. To make him
more mechanical, more arbitrary, more whimsical, more rigid,
more aloof, or more unstable than the best we see and value in
human personality is to be off on a train of theological thought
that is obviously and deeply heretical.

[7] *The Importance of Living* (New York: Reynal & Hitchcock, 1937),
p. 407.

CHAPTER FOUR

On Accepting the Universe

*T*HE nineteenth-century authoress, Margaret Fuller, is unfortunately not very well known by posterity, but she is famous for a remark made to Thomas Carlyle which is often quoted. "Yes," she said thoughtfully to Carlyle, "yes, I accept the universe." To which Carlyle is said to have replied, "By gad, you'd better." Miss Fuller, albeit somewhat reluctantly, was bearing witness to the Christian doctrine of creation. For all practical purposes the doctrine of creation comes down to this: that a man must accept the world as it is, the world of sticks and stones, of change and decay, of mud and stars, as the real world in which his destiny is to be achieved. Whatever dreams he may have of another and better world, he is called by God to take his place fully and responsibly in this one, for God is the source of this world and it is his purpose that man should find this world good.

This Christian acceptance of the universe has stood as a bulwark against a persistent tendency in human thought to despair of the physical and temporal world of ordinary human experience. The bulwark has, of course, not been absolutely impregnable. Even in the New Testament itself, the phrase "the world" is oftentimes used in a disparaging way. "For all that is in the world, the lust of the flesh, and the lust of the eye, and the pride of life, is not of the Father, but is of the world." (I John 2: 16). Both Protestantism and Catholicism have shared the uneasiness which the New Testament exhibits toward the world. The long history of monasticism, for example, with its insistence upon the renunciation of certain "natural" satisfactions is proof that accepting the universe doesn't just mean a relaxed enjoyment of life and nothing more. Monasticism has its counterpart in Protestantism in certain aspects of the Evangelical tradition and in Puritanism. Here is comparable rigor and austerity and suspicion of the comforts and pleasures of this life.

The Doctrine of Creation

Amidst all this, however, the doctrine of creation has nevertheless operated to limit the excesses of self-punishment and self-degradation that have sometimes passed as marks of superior piety among ascetic religions of the East. Christian orthodoxy in the doctrine of creation declares that the natural and the historical can be redeemed without being destroyed. This means that nothing in the created order of things is intrinsically evil, to be utterly rejected or completely renounced. Sexuality, wealth, power, physical health, comfort, beauty, art, learning—these are all things to be employed and used, taken up into some pattern of a full and rich life. For all its suspicions about the world, which we must look at more fully in a moment, Christianity nevertheless affirmed its essential suitability as a place for Christians to live out their destiny under God. This is all the more remarkable in view of the hostility that the world of the first and second century showed toward the Christians and of the widespread malaise of spirit that was felt among the more sensitive men and women of that period. One of the interests one feels in studying the writings of an intelligent early Christian like St. Augustine is to see how the doctrine of creation restrains his tendency to depreciate physical and material things. William Temple's dictum that Christianity is the most materialistic of the great world religions is probably true, and is an outpost of orthodoxy against the tendency to spiritualize religion and to render its teaching in an idealistic manner.

If the temptations to heresy in the first few centuries of the Christian era were toward a kind of spiritualism, there is a corresponding temptation in our own time to a kind of uncritical materialism which overlooks a genuine Christian uneasiness about the world that we have already noticed. There is too much in the New Testament and in Christian history about the dangers and the pitfalls to be found in the characteristic experiences of this world to be able to say, as some modern writers say, that since the world is God's creation it is without qualification good and to be thoroughly and unhesitatingly enjoyed. In the balance, orthodoxy would probably lean in that direction, but as in other fields of Christian doctrine, it *is* a question of balance that confronts us. C. S. Lewis has reminded us that the heresies which we like to belabor and condemn and from which we prefer to celebrate our freedom are the heresies of a generation other than our own. So in our time, there has been a great deal of condemnation of the errors of asceticism and Puritanism when as a matter of fact the last danger into which comfortable, middle-class American suburbanites are likely to fall is the excesses of hair-shirt monks or sabbatarian Puritans. The doctrine of creation is not the only Christian doctrine there is. It is well to read the sober second thoughts God has about the creation after the Fall in the Garden of Eden. "Cursed is the ground for thy sake; in sorrow shalt thou eat of it all the days of thy life. . . . In the sweat of thy face shalt thou eat bread, till thou return unto the ground; for out of it wast thou taken: for dust thou art and unto dust shalt thou return" (Genesis 3: 17, 19).

Man and the World of Nature

There is a long tradition both in the Bible and in Christian history of uneasiness about the world. The uneasiness obviously is not about the world as it essentially is, for that is ruled out by the doctrine of divine creation out of nothing (that is to say, entirely due to the creative purpose of God). Quite plainly, the uneasiness comes from an uneasiness about the world *as man uses it and lives in it.* "There's the rub." Man and the natural world—even more obviously, man and history—are in close relationship to one another, and the sin of man infects and distorts the whole created order. The Christian tradition warns us against "the pomps and vanities of this wicked world and all the sinful lusts of the flesh." The point is that man goes wrong precisely in his condition as a part of the animal and material creation and in the midst of culture and civilization and society. As we shall see when we come to consider man's sin, it is *not* purely spiritual. He does not decide in the abstract to be rebellious and selfish and wicked. That is the picture the Bible gives us of the sin of the devil, and while man's sin is something like the sin of the devil, there is an important difference. The difference is just this—that man is part of the material and social world, and so evil makes its appeal in those terms.

Just because man is an animal and needs food and shelter and clothing, he can be appealed to make the acquisition of all this the center and meaning of his existence. Just because man is social and needs approval and friendship and a sense of belonging, he can be appealed to to make the world his master and arbiter, and its standards and tastes the code by which he lives. The world and the flesh press their exaggerated claims upon us day and night, through the radio, television, advertising, and in a hundred other ways. It will not do just to say that the creation is essentially good and so man can relax and enjoy life without discipline or renunciation or any kind of self-denial. The ancient tradition of fasting in Lent and on Fridays has been too easily thrown overboard in the exciting celebration of the doctrine of creation, and of the corollary that only a positive approach toward life is consistent with Christian theology.

The Christian insight on creation is that of a potentially good thing always in danger of being distorted and corrupted by the perversity and self-assertiveness of man. This forbids us to feel entirely relaxed in "accepting the universe," but it also forbids us to flee from the world or from the obligations and responsibilities which life there entails. Even Christian monasticism in its developed form is closely related to the life of the world. The solitary recluse of the Egyptian desert gives way to the member of an organized monastic community busily employed in study, social service, and prayer, all of which have an eye to the world and its needs. St. Francis expresses this "world-affirming asceticism" in these words: "God hath called us into this holy religion [i.e., monasticism] for the salvation of the world, and has made this compact between the world and us, that we should give it good example and that it should provide for our necessities." [1] No Christian attitude toward ethics is orthodox that does not accept the situation in which man actually finds himself in creation and in history as the starting point of ethical responsibility. Christian love is not an abstract ideal which exists in some pure and absolute form and which can be related to life only through a series of compromises. To accommodate love to the particular situations in which its purposes are to be realized is not "compromising." Love is whatever action is strategic and helpful and edifying under the circumstances. That determination can only be made by a frank and realistic analysis of the actual situation. Politics, we have been told, is the art of the possible. The same thing might be said about Christian ethics. Christian love is not striking some pose or intending some good. It is positive, constructive, active good will, achieving its beneficent purpose within the limitations which the life of nature and history imposes. Amiable impracticality is no

[1] *The Little Flowers of St. Francis of Assisi,* tr. Dom Roger Hudleston (London: Burns Oates, 1953), p. 131.

Christian virtue; the injunction to be "wise as serpents" is sufficient evidence for that.

The Reality of Power

One of the fundamental facts of the creation is the
fact of power. In accepting the universe, Christians are obliged
to face the reality that nothing is done by wishing it were so or
by deciding that it ought to be so; it is done by the exercise of
power. One of the most persistent heresies is the idea that power
is something too indelicate for Christians to talk about, especially
social and political power. A depressing example of this heresy
was the spate of letters which came to *The Christian Century* in
1952 in response to a request as to suggestions for ending what
then appeared to be the stalemate of the Korean War. It would
be difficult to imagine a greater collection of eloquent irrelevancies.
It was urged that the United Nations withdraw all their troops
from South Korea and appeal to the conscience of the world to
urge the Communists to do the same! It was recommended that
our bombers stop delivering bombs on enemy lines and substitute
food parcels with messages about the blessings of peace! It is no
wonder that the picture of the average clergyman which appears
in popular novels, plays, and motion pictures is that of a completely impractical dreamer, living in an unreal world and flirting
around the edges of reality as a kind of comic relief. The phrase
"power politics" illustrates with what suspicion we regard power,
for that phrase is intended to describe the most ruthless and brutal
kind of compulsion, wholly lacking in any ethical concern whatever. But as Paul Tillich has pointed out, there is really no other
kind of politics but a politics which is concerned with the development and exercise of power. The most elementary observation
of the way the world operates would save a good deal of Christian exhortation and admonition from the terrible curse of futility
and irrelevance under which it so often operates.

The Confusion about "Natural Laws"

To recognize the reality of power and the ways in which it operates does not, however, imply that it is not to be consciously employed by the free will and decision of men. The universe in which we live is a universe in which men can and do exercise a very considerable freedom with respect to natural and social forces. "The laws of nature" are sometimes appealed to as if they were tyrannical prescriptions of human behavior. On this view, Christian ethics is not so much an adventure in decision and responsibility as it is a resignation to the way things must be. Again exaggeration has become heresy. There are, of course, observable patterns by which nature and history operate, but these are always subject to the play of man's deliberate decisions. There is something quite unjustified and arbitrary in condemning what is called "interference" with natural law. Men are always interfering with natural law. They do it every time they cut the front lawn or have a molar filled or take a trip in an airplane. They employ one natural process to counteract and modify the operation of another natural process.

Two recent examples of this heretical exaltation of the authority of natural law are found in the Roman Catholic attitude toward birth control and in the intransigent opposition of reactionary businessmen to political controls over economic life. In the first instance it is argued that natural law has established the procreation of children as the sole purpose of sexual relations. To frustrate this result by what are somewhat arbitrarily called "unnatural" means is supposedly an obvious defiance of natural law. The devotees of Adam Smith argue in a similar fashion. There are inviolate laws of nature which govern economic activity such as the law of supply and demand and the law of enlightened self-interest. To "interfere" with these laws by political regulation will bring some vague and dread punishment, as inevitable in its way as the punishment which comes to those who defy the law of gravitation. This is heresy as well as nonsense. Natural law is subject to the free and imaginative decisions of men. If man is to replenish and subdue the earth, he must obviously learn to play one natural process off against another for the sake of achieving purposes which nature herself would either not achieve at all or achieve only after interminable experiments of trial and error. In the case of economic life, it is plain from an examination of the facts that imaginative human devices such as the development of monopolies had already profoundly altered the operation of the laws of supply and demand long before political regulation was attempted. To "accept the universe" is to know whatever can be known about the way it operates but not to be bound by past experience or limited in imagination and adventurous experimentation by the concept of rigid laws which are really the fictions of cautious minds.

Miracles

The Christian doctrine of creation and of man's role as helping to direct and control it presupposes that it is an orderly creation. We have just looked at some exaggerations of the role of natural law, but there are some regular and predictable patterns and sequences of cause and effect which make it possible for man to predict with fair accuracy the outcome of his choices and decisions. If this were not so, then, of course, there would be an end to any sense of human responsibility at all. If as the consequence of careless driving one has a fatal accident, he cannot in an orderly universe excuse himself by shrugging his shoulders and saying deprecatingly, "Well, you never know, do you?" The answer is, "Of course you know. Certain ways of behavior carry certain consequences. It is your business to know enough about life to recognize and accept the common rules of cause and effect." This puts a limit, of course, upon the extent to which God can intervene and suspend the orderliness of the universe. To "accept the universe" means that in a very important sense one does not expect what is usually meant by a miracle. (Indeed, a miracle that is expected is probably not, strictly speaking, a miracle at all.)

One must say "what is usually meant by a miracle," because miracle can be defined either in a loose and general way or in a precise and logical way. In the loose usage of common speech, a miracle is anything that was not expected. "I think it's a miracle he recovered" really means we expected he would die. Life is full of such miracles. In some periods of history when men have exaggerated their powers of prediction and their knowledge of immutable natural laws, miracles have constituted a challenging intellectual problem. "Here is something we have not predicted or understood. How can there be such things in a world where we have mastered all the laws and foreseen all the possibilities?" The answer has usually been that such things represent the special intervention of God into an otherwise tidy and predictable universe.

There is a more precise and logical way of speaking about miracles. David Hume called a miracle "a violation of a law of nature by a particular volition of the Deity." A modern writer, Mr. C. S. Lewis, offers a similar definition: "an invasion of the psycho-physical universe by an uncreated and unconditioned reality." In this strict sense, it is probably not really a miracle that our friend recovered when we expected him to die. It is just that we did not know enough about his condition and about the drugs and medicines and therapy being used to cure him, in order to make an accurate prediction. Here is a difficult question about a miracle: how accurate can anyone's prediction about the future be? Doctors and physicians make better predictions than most other people about the prospects for physical recovery of a patient, but they have been surprisingly wrong on occasions. Are all such occasions "miraculous"? How do we know when one of Mr. Lewis's rather militaristically conceived "invasions of the psycho-physical universe" takes place? The answer seems to be that one is never quite certain that he has a real miracle, in the precise way of speaking, on his hands. There are the usual patterns by which things happen, and then there are unexpected things which seem to break away from the pattern. The latter are always interesting, exciting, sometimes even awesome, but it is never entirely possible to say whether some "immutable" law has been violated or whether a divine "invasion" has taken place. It is only important that both the regularities and the irregularities be seen as under the power of God and signs of his providence and ever-present activity.

To be agnostic in this way about miracles is not the same thing as to say they could never take place. To assert the latter would seem to imply (according to whether one is speaking loosely or precisely about miracles) either that nothing unexpected could happen or that God never varies his obedience of his own laws. The first is absurd; the second is presumptuous. The world is filled with astonishing and awesome events. The very presence of free men in the world, moving and acting upon the course of events, is a guarantee that the unexpected will keep on occurring. The Christian assumption that behind all things is a personal God would lead a Christian to be even more receptive to the possibility of the occurrence of the miraculous. Some recent theologians have been disposed to read God's mind and come to the conclusion that under no circumstances would he disrupt the routine of the universe. The late Douglas C. McIntosh of Yale gave God the benefit of a New Haven sense of the fitness of things by declaring: "There is no place in the best possible kind of world for the arbitrary interruption of the established natural order." [2] But even men for good reasons interrupt the orderly sequence of their affairs for the sake of a higher purpose. C. S. Lewis has suggested that God may be like a skillful poet who, although he knows well enough the laws of rhyme and meter, may occasionally deviate slightly from the rule for the sake of special effect. It would be a dreary and intolerable sort of family in which rules were rigidly obeyed without any variation or spontaneous surprises.

A Latin phrase which has sometimes been used with respect

[2] D. C. McIntosh, *The Reasonableness of Christianity* (New York: Chas. Scribner's Sons, 1925), p. 98.

to miracles goes: *Potuit, decuit, ergo fecit* (He could, it was fitting, therefore he did it). There are many things wrong with this as a guide for understanding miracles, but for the moment we are concerned with *decuit* (it was fitting). This argument is often used, but it appears to be too subjective to carry much weight. Dr. McIntosh would say that it is never fitting to interrupt the established order. Roman Catholics find it fitting that the Mother of the Incarnate Lord should from the moment of her conception be free from the taint of original sin. Most Protestants don't find it fitting at all. A friend of mine used to say he thought the Virgin Birth entirely fitting on Christmas Eve, but the rest of the year he was not so sure. To argue that it would be appropriate and suitable for God to perform some miracle is to put too much weight on the fragile foundation of personal preference and impression. Suitability is no criterion at all for determining whether miracles ever happen and certainly no proof that any specific miracle did actually occur.

The Real Problem about Miracles

The real problem about miracles is the evidence as to whether any particular one really took place. At this point our Latin phrase *ergo, fecit* (therefore he did it) is most seriously misleading. A statement of possibility and an expression of personal preference carries no "therefore" with it at all. Whether any specific miracle occurred is a matter of evidence. One will be persuaded by the force of the evidence or not persuaded because of the lack of force, but mere possibility and suitability carry no weight whatsoever. The logical fallacy here is widespread in the modern Church. It is often said that while the evidence for the Virgin Birth story in the Gospels is ambiguous, nevertheless one must believe that it happened because the doctrine fits in so well with the conviction that Jesus Christ was the Son of God. There is no sense in that kind of an argument at all. One can only put credence in the story of the Virgin Birth insofar as the Gospel and New Testament evidence permits *and no farther*. If the evidence is ambiguous, then the only choice for the Christian believer is to be somewhat tentative and agnostic too. Of course, if one can persuade himself that the New Testament affords strong evidence of the Virgin Birth, he is justified in holding strongly that it occurred, but on no other grounds than the evidence itself.

The Nature of Christian Faith

This will perhaps sound heretical to many readers, and the next book that comes out on "Modern Heresies" may include the last paragraph as a horrible example! What is at stake here is the nature of Christian faith. It is not, as we have said previously, mere intellectual opinion. It is a commitment of the self to that which gives central meaning and controlling direction to life. Can the question of the biological process by which Jesus Christ came into human life possibly be of this order of importance? The question the Christian asks is not the question of biological detail but the question of religious significance. Because he who was born—no matter by what process—was the Son of God himself, I can put my trust in him for life and for death. The test of orthodoxy is whether a theological statement is consistent with this central Christian experience. Statements about the Virgin Birth as a biological fact, whether in favor or opposed, miss the religious point altogether. Like St. Augustine we should say that the world is full of portents and wonders, awesome events that remind us of human weakness and of the reality of divine power and meaning in life. It would not be surprising if the supreme event in man's religious history, the coming into history of the God-man in Person, were accompanied by unusual and astounding occurrences. The evidence for them as historic events may be weak, but insofar as they point to the religious significance of the great central event they are true in a deeper sense than historically true. Such events are meant to prompt us to wonder and awe and trust and faith. It is a serious heresy to misuse the events of the Bible as if they were given us for statements of sober fact, to which we might or might not respond by saying, "How interesting." They are given us that we might say with St. Thomas, "My Lord and my God."

Spiritual Healing

In these days something additional has to be said about the matter of spiritual or Christian healing, since it is a movement that is widely spread throughout the contemporary Church. Like any other popular movement it may be distorted by false theological understanding, and indeed some of the most articulate sponsors of the movement have been notoriously careless in what they have promised for it. Following our general principle of "accepting the universe," the Christian can never pretend that sickness isn't real and powerful. Malfunctioning of the body, cancer cells, virus, germs—these play a large part in the operations of the world in which we live, and their presence and strength cannot be questioned by anyone who pretends to accept the world realistically.

Nor, of course, can anyone question the countervailing power of medicines and surgery and other forms of therapy. "The Lord hath created medicines out of the earth," says the apocryphal book of Ecclesiasticus, "and he that is wise will not abhor them" (Ecclesiasticus 38: 4). It is surely a heresy which undermines the doctrine of creation to equate piety with the avoidance of the practice of medical science. Modern healing sects that dogmatically reject medicine would logically be obliged to reject food for the same reason. It is perhaps not accidental that the scientific study and practice of medicine has flourished wherever the biblical doctrine of creation has been influential. One of the signs that God's ultimate will for man is health and wholeness of personality is the presence of healing medicines in the earth and the presence in the heart of man of the urge to employ every skill and every physical balm and cure for the healing of his fellows.

The spiritual healing movement in modern Christianity has a valid point to make in emphasizing the close knit unity of body and soul. As we shall see further when we think about the heretical notions that are abroad today about the nature of man, this recognition of the physical basis of human personality is a distinctively biblical idea and a sharp contrast to the spiritualistic view of man in many nonbiblical religions. It is a view which has received impressive confirmation from the modern investigations into the psychosomatic nature of disease and of effective therapy. It is no surprise to a Christian who understands the orthodox doctrine of man to learn that disorders of mind and soul can wreak havoc in the human body. When a man's soul is wrong, when he tries to live life on his own strength without any confidence about God and about God's love and care, when he is desperately and anxiously seeking to establish his own reputation and build up his own defenses against a hostile and menacing universe, then that man is almost surely going to manifest signs of disorder in his physical body. And the corollary is also true. When a man puts his life into God's hands, when he trusts God's mercy and power and leaves off depending on his own wit and his own strength, then through such an act of faith he releases restorative and healing powers which medicine may not be able to identify or define but which it respects and welcomes.

The Church's ministry to the sick is more than just a ministry of resignation or, even worse, a suitable prelude for the undertaker's visit. It is a ministry of healing, and the current interest in this aspect of the Church's pastoral responsibility is an overdue correction of a long-standing neglect. That it is a revival of an ancient practice and not a novelty is proved by the most cursory examination of the Church's history. A seventeenth-century Canon of the Church of England wisely said,

We strictly charge and command all physicians that when they shall be called to sick persons, they first of all admonish and persuade them to send for the physicians of souls, that after provision hath been made for the spiritual health of the soul, they may the more hopefully proceed to the use of corporal medicine. For when the cause is taken away, the effect may follow.[3]

The heresy which lurks behind this otherwise welcome revival of Christian healing is the unwillingness to accept the inevitability of death. Some day every man has to face an experience of sickness or infirmity from which he will not recover. It is an experience, the Bible says, which is somehow related to man's sinfulness, for it is only after the Fall in the Genesis story that the curse of death is allowed to establish its power over man's existence. The Church has never clearly defined how or why this is so. Perhaps death is allowed to have its temporary victory over sinful men in order to remind them of the foolishness of their pretension and pride. However man may play at being god, strutting and boasting of his power, conquering specific diseases and removing many human limitations, nevertheless there stands a final sentence upon his life: it will come to an end. "In the midst of life we are in death." "Accepting the universe" requires a frank recognition that any healing ministry, whether by medicine or psychiatry or spiritual means, has a limitation put upon it. It is frustrated at the grave. It is cruel and dangerous heresy to deny this inevitability or, which amounts to the same thing, to insist that every disease can be cured if the patient is spiritually mature enough. The Church's ministry to the sick may in former times have been too insistent upon a mood of resignation. It is surely heretical, however, to counteract this by a conspiracy of silence about death as if every one to whom the clergy were ministering were bound to recover.[4]

[3] Cf. P. E. More and F. L. Cross, *Anglicanism* (London: S. P. C. K., 1935), p. 521.
[4] The Service for the Visitation of the Sick in the proposed new Book of Common Prayer seems to reflect this lack of realism. The admirable prayer which contains the phrase "make us deeply sensible of the shortness and uncertainty of human life," has been eliminated. An inquiry to the Commission brought the curious reply that a special service in preparation for death was contemplated. But surely every sickness ought to be regarded as a reminder of the inevitability of death. Will it not be a rather delicate decision when to pray for recovery and when to turn the page to the section designed to prepare for death?

The Fulfillment of the Created Order

"Accepting the universe" widens the area of Christian concern to include everything which God has made, which man has spoiled and which Christ proposes to redeem. Archbishop William Temple identified as one of the most persistent modern heresies the idea that God is primarily interested in religion. "He is not," said the Archbishop. "He is interested in life." The doctrine of creation implied that meaning and purpose can be discovered and realized in every aspect of the material, temporal world. The whole creation, St. Paul says, is groaning and travailing in pain, frustrated in its efforts to realize the divine purpose inherent in it. That is a vivid image. It would say that the very wood of a rotting city slum cries out against the misuse to which it is put by human sin, that the air suffers under the burden of contamination by atomic fall-out. God's creation can be frustrated. That is one of the possibilities inherent in human freedom. When man is redeemed the whole created order has new opportunities for fulfillment and realization.

The Church would be well-advised to be modest in her claims to supervise and direct the processes of human activity by which this fulfillment and realization take place. In the eagerness of the modern Church to counteract the heresy of pietism, which sees God as concerned only with what men do on their knees in church, there have been extravagant claims made about the profound difference which Christian perspective introduces into human thought and action.[5] Many so-called Christian insights are so wide-

[5] The author recalls the irritation of some non-Christian college faculty at this phrase in George F. Thomas's pamphlet, "Religious Perspectives on College Teaching" (published by the Edward W. Hazen Foundation, New Haven, 1952): "The natural scientist who is a Christian will see in nature all that his secular colleague sees; but he will look upon it with eyes filled with wonder and awe, because he believes that it is the product of divine power and wisdom rather than blind chance" (p. 13). "Are wonder and awe ruled out for non-Christian scientists?" asked these critics. A careful reading of Professor Thomas might have disarmed these objectors, but the incident reveals how hard it is to trace Christian influence and how modest it behooves the Church to be.

spread in our culture that even though they may be Christian in origin, it is presumptuous to claim them in our time as a Christian monopoly. It is very doubtful whether one ought to talk about Christian sociology or Christian politics or Christian art, any more than one talks about Christian plumbing or Christian arithmetic. There are, one is grateful to say, Christian sociologists and Christian politicians, not to mention Christian plumbers and Christian accountants. The Church does not prescribe their methodology nor dictate their conclusions. The Church does provide a setting of ultimate insight and confident assurance about the validity of life's tasks by its doctrines of the creation, the fall, the redemption, and the life of the world to come. Against this background men and women in their several callings seek to realize the divine purpose in politics, in art, in business, in science, and indeed in every area of human activity.

The Christian orthodoxy about creation invites man to the creative and redemptive use of every aspect, every power, every reality in the physical and material and temporal order. His eye is turned toward this world, for it is only by looking discriminatingly and accurately at this world that he can perceive the unseen and eternal world. The Christian doctrine about creation does not, as we have seen, imply an undiscriminating reverence for life which relaxes into an enjoyment of all created things just as they are. There are issues and purposes to be fulfilled and realized by positive and constructive action. The Christian looks into and through the created order to find the eternal order. He does not seek the eternal by turning his face away from the temporal. "Accepting the universe" means believing that this strange, fascinating, mysterious, and endlessly varied world is precisely the setting in which God asks us to discover the meaning and purpose of our existence and to realize those possibilities of freedom and responsibility, of faith and service, for which he created us.

CHAPTER FIVE

More or Less a Beast

*T*HE difficulty is to decide what man is and what he wants to be. In his charming but disconcerting novel *You Shall Know Them,* the French writer Vercors (Jean Bruller) has shown how troublesome it is to try to define humanity. He imagines a party of anthropologists discovering strange animal-men on a remote Pacific island, and the problem is raised as to whether they are a species of ape or a kind of primitive man. How does one know? What precisely is the borderline between the two? Finally a Parliamentary Committee recommends that they be adjudged to be human inasmuch as they had "shown signs of a spirit of religion." "What is man?" the Psalmist asked thousands of years ago. Of all the questions man puts to himself this has proved to be the most stubborn. Orthodox Christianity has defined a way to answer the question, and this more than almost any other aspect of traditional theology has captured the interest of modern thinkers.

One way to answer the question "What is man?" is to say that he is the only creature who would think of asking such a question about himself. As we saw in our discussion of the Trinity, being a human person means reflecting upon oneself, making oneself the object of thought and judgment and discrimination. This capacity and the sense of responsibility and freedom which it entails make man what he is. This is what theologians mean by the soul. The soul is not some tiny part of the person, like an appendix, the existence of which can be debated. The soul is proved not by dissection but by man's power, which he exercises all the time, to stand over against himself and think and plan and dream about his existence and his destiny. There is a fancy word for this uniquely human power; it is "self-transcendence." It is the source of man's special dignity; it is the source of his deepest misery and anxiety. Because of it, he can imagine himself to be greater than he really is. Indeed as we saw in another chapter he can pretend that he is number one in the universe, whereas he is really closer probably to number 100 trillion. On the other hand, he can imagine and execute forms of behavior which although we call them "bestial" most animals would be ashamed to be found doing.

The "Divine Spark" Heresy

This soul of man is made in the image of God. That means that man's self-consciousness, his ability to conceive purposes and realize ambitions, his self-transcendence are something like God's personal life. (We have already seen with what reservations this must be said.) One sometimes hears it said that all men have a spark of divinity in them. It is not quite clear what that means. If it means that some aspect of human life—man's power of reasoning, for example—is a part of the divine life of God himself, then it is wrong and heretical. This understanding of man's relationship to God is one which is characteristically found in Stoic writers of the first three centuries.[1] The biblical doctrine is that

[1] Cf. Epictetus in his *Discourses,* Book II, chapter 8, "You are a fragment of God; you have within you a part of him. Why then are you ignorant of your kinship? . . . Whenever you mix in society, whenever you take physical exercise, whenever you converse, do you not know that you are nourishing God, exercising God?"

man is not divine, or semi-divine, or partly divine. He is an animal who because of his self-transcendence can either come into relationship with God or can consciously reject God's offer and invitation to that relationship. To suppose that all men had some part of the divine nature within themselves would make it difficult to explain the less attractive aspects of human behavior. What happened to the divine spark in the Nazis who exterminated hundreds of thousands of Jews in gas chambers? If one answers that the spark was thoroughly suppressed in such people, the reply would seem to be that the divine spark appears to be too easily quenchable to be in any way a part of the power and glory of God himself. Human nature is able to stand against God and resist him forever. As we shall see later, that is what the doctrine of hell means. It is impossible to hold this doctrine and believe at the same time that man is somehow inherently divine. This latter idea, as St. Augustine once pointed out, leads men to trust in their own natural powers and undermines the kind of dependence upon God which constitutes the real meaning of living in the divine image.[2]

Another disadvantage of the "divine spark" heresy is that it divides man in two. The divine part of him is supposed to exist only accidentally alongside the rest of him, and the two are only casually related, and seem to have no fundamental influence on each other. The soul, on this theory, is related to the body as the body is related to a suit of clothes or as a person is related to a house in which he lives.[3] I can change my clothes without making any serious or profound changes in my personality. I can move from one house to another and still be essentially the same person.

[2] Professor Paul Ramsey [cf. *Basic Christian Ethics* (New York: Chas. Scribner's Sons, 1951), p. 256] quotes Augustine as follows: "There was danger lest the human mind . . . should be thought to be of the same nature with him who created it, and should fall away by pride from him to whom it should be united by love. For the mind becomes like God to the extent vouchsafed by its subjection of itself to him." This means that the "image of God" in man is something achieved, not something immutably given.
[3] One recognizes this heretical implication in a title like this one of Professor William Ernest Hocking, "The Self: Its Body and Freedom." That sounds as if the self could exist quite independently of its body, which is heretical on the Christian theory.

This heresy had substantial support in the third-century Church from the important Church Father, Origen. Origen imagined two creations of man (he was acute enough to see that there were two accounts of man's creation in Genesis and built his theory upon this fact):

At the creation of man . . . there was first created the man that was "after the image" in whom there was nothing material. He who was in the image was not made out of matter . . . And when God made man he did not take the dust of the earth as he did the second time, but he made him in the image of God. That that which is in the image of God is understood as immaterial and superior to all corporeal existence . . . by the apostle is shown by his words, as follows: (Colossians iii, verse 9,) "putting off the old man . . . and putting on the new." [4]

Man: Body and Soul

The Christian doctrine of the relationship of body and soul is not so casual as that. The body was not a divine afterthought—and, as Origen seemed to think, an unfortunate one at that. Man cannot be man until he is fully created as a union of soul and body. His soul is not some independent entity that moves into bodies and out again without anything essentially happening to it. The soul and the body exist together necessarily, and together they identify the personal self. Popular superstition to the contrary, Bridey Murphy cannot "return" in another body and still be the old Bridey we knew back in Ireland! A little exercise in imagination may help to persuade the doubtful reader. Try to imagine what your mother or your husband or anyone else you care about deeply is like, without picturing any physical or material characteristics at all. It cannot be done. The self whom you love is inseparable from a light in the eye, an inflection of the voice, a characteristic posture of the body. As we saw when we were considering "accepting the universe," man's life is rooted in nature and history. It is through

[4] Origen, "Dialogue with Heraclides," Chapter 146, in *Alexandrian Christianity*, ed. by H. Chadwick and J. F. L. Oulton (Philadelphia: Westminster Press, 1954), p. 448.

his body and the material and temporal setting in which his body exists that he lives and fulfills himself. Christianity's picture of man is not of a semi-divine soul that has unfortunately and inexplicably become involved in the enmeshing frustrations of time and matter, from which frustrations he seeks to be freed that he may become once more his essentially spiritual self. God took dust and made man in his image in one indivisible operation, Origen to the contrary notwithstanding. That means that the destiny of man is to be worked out here and now in the midst of fleshly historical existence, which is to say, by accepting the universe and not by hankering after a purely spiritual world which has no connection with this one.

It is perhaps not surprising that this complex and potentially very unstable being, poised between two orders of life, should go wrong. Here is an animal who is nevertheless so much more than an animal that he knows his limitations and can seek to overcome them. Like God he can project great ideals and purposes, but unlike God he is caught in a particular time and place with all the limitations that carries with it and he knows that these limitations will finally prevail against him in death. Man is potentially an explosive being, and the third chapter of Genesis is the classical description of how the explosion takes place. Here we meet the doctrine of original sin, a doctrine as vigorously fought over as almost any other in Christian history, a doctrine which because it has been so appreciatively rediscovered in recent years is one of the most debatable in contemporary Christianity. What are orthodoxy and heresy here? The answer can be given only with great caution and hesitation, for we are living in the midst of this theological debate.

The Doctrine of Man in Genesis

The Genesis story itself is the origin of the myth of the Fall, and we must look at the story to get our bearings. Before we do, however, we must dispose of the contention that the third chapter of Genesis tells us of the historical event which is the origin of original sin. It has been fashionable to think that Darwin's discoveries about the origin of species made the Garden of Eden story impossible except as material for perfume advertisements and slightly salacious stories. Christianity has no interest in whether the story of Genesis 3 is historical or not. Indeed, an examination of the story itself, as we shall see in a moment, suggests that it could not possibly have happened historically. A recent cartoon in the *New Yorker* magazine shows a spaceship landing on another planet, and the two men who emerge see a blissfully naked young lady under a fruit tree, listening to a snake, and reaching out to pick one of the fruits, while a complacent and indulgent male companion looks on. One of the men is rushing up to them, shouting, "Just a moment. We have something to tell you." The humor lies in the impossibility of such a scene ever taking place.[5] The Garden of Eden is a picture of the way sin always expresses itself. It happens every day in a thousand ways and in innumerable situations. It can only be taken seriously as an historical event if we suppose that all men descended from the first two parents who took part in the original tragedy, and modern science, although very tentative in its conclusions, does not necessarily suppose that human life is all derived from two original human beings, but speculates that it may be derived from several "original parents" who emerged in different places and different times. There can be no planet where human beings do not know original sin. Wherever man appears in his unique nature as an animal in the image of God, sin is a quality of his existence, unless and until God in Christ has won his faith and his Spirit has captured his heart.

[5] Unfortunately, Mr. C. S. Lewis in an otherwise useful pamphlet, *Will We Lose God in Outer Space?* (Forward Movement Publications, Cincinnati), has seriously supposed that there may be human beings in the universe who have never been affected by original sin, because there may not have been a Garden of Eden scene or its equivalent on the planet where they live! E. L. Mascall in *The Importance of Being Human* (New York: Columbia University Press, 1957) also seems to believe that important issues are at stake in asserting the historicity of the first sin. In these cases, as we shall see, the intention is to affirm the distinction between essential man and his subsequent sinful state. Whatever may be one's view of this distinction, it cannot be maintained by treating Genesis as in any way reliable history.

Cosmic Evil

At the outset the story of the Fall introduces us to the reality of what might be called cosmic evil. The trouble begins when the serpent proposes defiance and disobedience. Whatever the authors and compilers of Genesis thought this serpent was, it has been customary in later Christian thought to identify him with Satan, the fallen angel who fights against God. Christian orthodoxy has never attempted to define dogmatically the nature of cosmic evil, although the picturesque tradition of the devil and his angels has kept Christians aware of its power and reality. Most modern Christians will not find it profitable to speculate on the existence of a personal devil, but they ought to meditate seriously on the experiences which have led men to posit such a being. Sin is an ongoing program in the universe long before you or I appear on the scene. It is in the air. It has embedded itself in the social institutions and customs by which we live. St. Paul spoke about "spiritual wickedness in high places," and he meant not corruption in Washington but a bias toward evil in the very heart of things. This is a view of life which, until quite recently, modern people have found it difficult to comprehend. They have supposed that evil was the result of individual wrong decisions. If a man was wicked the thing to do was to tell him to stop it at once. The picture of "this world with devils filled" was, for modern men, a superstition that had no contemporary meaning at all.

More recent history and more recent investigations in psychology have made it apparent that the old imagery of the devil and his angels abroad in the world expressed profound truth. German Christians who had to wrestle with Naziism found that evil was a vast and permeating power that laid hold of men almost without their knowledge or consent. "The Prince of darkness grim" became a powerful symbol of a social reality which no one could resist except by some more powerful spiritual compulsion. The same truth was discovered in psychological analysis. It is not possible to say to someone suffering from psychological disorder, "Pull your-self together." There is a power and a dynamism in the personal life which can only be met and counteracted by an even more powerful and compelling force. The world in which we live is a dynamic one. It is not lying placidly inert waiting for us to do some-thing about it. It is a world of forces and powers which are on the move and which often draw men into their orbit and influence. Man is the victim of these forces oftentimes as much as he is their willing tool.

Original Sin: Man's Self-centredness

Why does man yield himself so often and so willingly to the powers of evil that assail and tempt him? Why does the suggestion to defy God find such an easy beachhead in the heart and mind of man? Genesis says the answer is complex and many-sided. For one thing, man is tempted to make himself God precisely be-cause he is something like God. Because he can imagine himself to be greater than he is—number one in the universe—he can pretend that his imaginations can be realized. It is his power to conceive purposes and fulfill ambitions that tempts him to try the greatest trick of all—to make himself the center of the universe. As Arch-bishop Temple once pointed out, this self-centredness of man is the inevitable consequence of the fact that each man does look out at the world from the perspective of his own location at the center. The newborn baby is aware of the world only as it impinges upon his existence. The mother, for example, is there to feed and support and keep him warm. That is not, of course, altogether true. The mother is a person in her own right. She does not exist just for the sake of the baby's comfort and happiness. So the baby begins life under the burden of a terrible distortion of reality. He thinks the world exists for his sake, and as he sits in his playpen, grabbing toys and demanding attention, he is the perfect model of sinful self-centredness. The spectacle is mildly amusing to us, partly because the incongruity between the tiny strength and the imperious demand is so great. But babies in playpens grow up to be dictators in chancelleries, and the prospect is somewhat less amusing, although essentially the sinful self-centredness is the same.

As we saw, however, in a previous chapter, man's self-centredness is expressed in terms of genuine needs which he seeks to satisfy. The genius of the Garden of Eden myth is shown in the fact that although the serpent's real temptation is to be as gods, he suggests that the defiance take the form of satisfying a perfectly natural human appetite and eating the forbidden fruit. "After all," Eve may be imagined to have said to herself, "a person needs a new taste sensation once in a while. This may be just the combination of vitamins and low-caloric content that my diet needs. I cannot tell what I'm missing until I try it." Man finds a plausible reason for his rebellion in the physical and social needs of his existence. He can always imagine satisfactions of those needs which are not at the moment being provided. Everyone supposes that he needs more than he really does in order to live effectively. It is a commonplace of recent economic history that the unbelievable luxuries of one generation become the indispensable necessities of the next. Man's freedom and imagination burden him with a restless desire for satisfactions that are always beyond his grasp. He can always picture more comfort, more security, more popularity, more success than are his at the moment, and so he sets out aggressively and self-confidently to seize them.

Inherent in this restlessness is the suspicion that God isn't doing as much for us as we might do for ourselves. The ability to imagine an infinite list of new satisfactions is coupled with a lingering anxiety that God may not allot me my fair share—a share which I tend to overestimate rather generously. Christianity does not disparage a reasonable prudence about one's own security and needs, but the point is that man is so unstable that "reasonable" is an almost impossible guide for his behavior. There is a dynamic and explosive will which works within man, always tending to go beyond what another observer would call "reasonable" and to become what the Litany calls "inordinate and sinful." The opposite of this sinful anxiety is the mood of St. Paul when he writes that he has learned to be content in whatever state of life he finds himself. Such a mood grows out of a realization that as Jesus said, "Your heavenly Father knoweth that ye have need of all these things." The line is hard to draw, but in theory it can be drawn between reasonable foresight and that driving anxiety about security, status, and privilege which betrays a lack of any kind of faith in God's providence and care. It has been said that unbelief is the first step in sin. When a man begins to doubt God's goodness and providential care, he is on his own in life, and the driving energy with which he pursues his own interests makes him heedless of anyone else.

Emil Brunner has described the complexity of the origin of sin in a memorable phrase: "It is a fruit that attracts; it is a whispered doubt that stirs; it is the dream of being like God that turns the scale." [6] This is the dynamism of sin, and whether or not Adam and Eve ever took that fatal taste in their garden paradise the story of the third chapter of Genesis has profound truth. The trouble with the story is that it simplifies matters a little too easily, for, someone may ask, can man really be free until he knows the possibility of good and evil? The Garden of Eden situation sounds a little dull when you think about it. The English writer H. H. Munro, usually known as Saki, attempted to write a little story of what it would be like if Eve had refused to eat the apple. She is depicted as a terrifyingly unimaginative dullard, who replies to all the temptations (God is finally reduced to plaguing the garden with mildew and caterpillar, and only the forbidden fruit looks appetizing), "No, we were told not to eat it, and we're not going to." [7] Placid, obedient man, without enough curiosity to want to know good and evil, is not a very attractive picture. If you miss the rebellion, you miss half of man's grandeur and splendor. The Christian ideal is not the placid innocency of Saki's Eve; it is the Second Adam, who knowing all there is to know about evil rejects it con-

[6] *Man in Revolt,* trans. by Olive Wyon (New York: Chas. Scribner's Sons, 1939), p. 132.
[7] *The Short Stories of Saki,* Introd. by Christopher Morley (New York: Viking Press, 1941), pp. 691-693.

sciously and deliberately by fulfilling all the possibilities of human nature in goodness. There never was a pre-Fall Adam. To be man is to be free, creative, inquiring, daring, imagining. Unfortunately, these exciting qualities of the human spirit are driven by a proud self-centredness that corrupts and destroys them. The angels and the flaming sword make it clear that man is not intended, however, to forswear his knowledge and strive to re-enter paradise. It cannot be done. Once man has eaten of the fruit of the knowledge of good and evil he is launched into a life of responsibility and self-consciousness from which there is no turning back.

There is a persistent heresy that equates sanctity with innocency. In a propaganda piece for Moral Re-armament a few years back there appeared—after a series of apocalyptic pictures showing some of the woes of modern life such as aerial bombing of cities, racial violence, labor disputes, etc.—a picture of a five-year-old child holding up an expectant hand, and under the picture were the words: "She knows the answer." That is not the Christian ideal. Christ bids men be wise as serpents, and it is clear from this passage that he does not mean to extol children for their innocence but for other qualities of spirit. Children do not hold the key to all of life's fulfillment and meaning. St. Paul's words—"when I became a man I put away childish things"—suggest that the Christian ideal is one of mature responsibility and shrewd wisdom, all at the service of a trusting and obedient will.

Total Depravity

Christianity says that the consequences of the Fall are catastrophic for human life and human institutions. Some theologians have used a much misunderstood phrase to describe how bad things are: total depravity. Much of the argument that has gone on over this phrase quite misses the point of it. John Calvin, who is usually taken to be the chief representative of those who hold this supposedly pessimistic view of human nature, makes it quite clear in one passage at least that he does not at all entertain the view that man loses his distinctive character as a result of the Fall.[8] The very power to sin, that is, to conceive of oneself as the center of existence, is due to the power of imagination and self-transcendence that we have already identified as the distinguishing mark of what it means to be a man. "Total depravity" properly means that everything man does apart from Christ is infected and corrupted by the distorted vision of self-centredness. There is no part of him, no faculty, no power in him that is not stained and twisted by this pride and self-aggressiveness. Anything man does betrays in some way his alienation from his true destiny and dignity. If total depravity meant that man ceased altogether to exercise the distinctive human function of self-judgment and self-criticism, then it would be a logical contradiction, for man would be so depraved that he could never guess that he was depraved. The Psalmist who cried out, "There is no righteous man left, no, not one," forgot about himself. That is a tribute to his humility, but it is a fault in his logic. Amos proclaimed the total apostasy of Israel and Judah, but he forgot the fact that he himself and the little band of his followers constituted at least a few exceptions to his universal pessimism.

Admittedly, there is a wave of disillusionment about man which has swept many modern writers and thinkers into a depth of despair over humanity, which is heretical because it denies the possibility that even through God's saving and redeeming action any significant and worthwhile human response can be made. A newspaper reporter once asked Tennessee Williams, "Why don't you write about nice people? Don't you know any nice people?" The playwright's reply is not recorded, but it can be assumed that his conviction is that in the psychologically diseased and deformed

[8] *Institutes,* Book II, chapter ii, section 12: "Some sparks continue to shine in the nature of man, even in its corrupt and degenerate state, which prove him to be a rational creature and different from the brutes, because he is endued with understanding; and yet . . . this light is smothered by so much ignorance; that it cannot act with any degree of efficiency. So the will being inseparable from the nature of man is not annihilated; but it is fettered by depraved and inordinate desire, so that it cannot aspire after anything that is good."

people who move through his plays one can see epitomized a gen-eralized sickness that afflicts all men. This is useful and sobering, because as we shall see presently, modern man's tendency has usually been to overemphasize his power and freedom. We ought to face up squarely to the fact that many of the modern plays and novels that seem so sordid correspond all too closely to the twisted and broken lives that many people live. But Christianity would insist that all this is a perversion and a misuse of essentially good human powers. Man's persistent abuse of his freedom must not obscure the fact that sin is a proof of God's image in man. Only a being who was created in God's image would dream of trying to usurp God's place. This is what Roman Catholic theology has tried to say by insisting that man's fundamental nature was not affected by the Fall.[9] Protestantism has usually rejected this distinction be-tween man's nature and man's existence and by the use of the phrase "total depravity" has declared that everything man does—even in the exercise of his distinctively human powers such as reason—shows the effects of sin. A recent semipopular statement of the Catholic view by the Anglican Dr. E. L. Mascall[10] insists, "Nevertheless, his fundamental natural endowments remain. He can make intellectual progress . . . the astounding scientific move-ment of the last four centuries is the most striking example of this." But can one isolate this scientific progress and regard it as wholly good apart from the uses and consequences of it? Has this scientific movement not led men to conceive of life—as we saw in Chapter Two—as an exercise in manipulation? Has it not produced a pre-occupation with material things and the consequent loss of a sense of the mysteries of love and faith and the other qualities that emerge in human relationships? The spectacle of the Nazi scientist experimenting with human beings proves that intellectual achieve-

[9] Cf. Thomas Aquinas, *Summa Theologica,* 12 ae, Q.85, Art. 1: "The con-stitution of human nature is neither destroyed nor diminished by sin." Quoted in *Nature and Grace,* ed. A. M. Fairweather (Philadelphia: West-minster Press, 1954), p. 128.
[10] *The Importance of Being Human* (New York: Columbia University Press, 1958), p. 87.

ment is not altogether free from corrupting and brutalizing tendencies. If Catholic theology about man is trying to identify some uncontaminated zone in his life and activity, the attempt seems to fly in the face of the evidence. As a matter of speculative theory it is true that man's nature is not destroyed by the Fall. As a matter of practical life everything man does has seeds of sin within it. Article XIII of the Anglican Thirty-nine Articles reflects this realistic analysis: "Works done before [or, it might be said, apart from] the grace of Christ and the Inspiration of his Spirit, are not pleasant to God . . . we doubt not but they have the nature of sin." This is a "hard saying" for a generation that has prided itself on its intellectual, scientific, political, and social accomplishments. It corresponds, however, to the widespread sense of revulsion and disillusionment felt by writers and thinkers and artists and often by the common man at the kind of world the last four centuries with their "astounding scientific movement" have produced.

The Heresy of Pelagius

Christian orthodoxy about man has pictured him as the victim of limitations and frustrations that arise out of this desperate attempt of his to establish himself at the center of life. The determination of this orthodoxy was the work of St. Augustine in his discussions and debates with Pelagius. It is difficult to expound the views of Pelagius without feeling a sympathetic surge of approval from a twentieth-century audience. He says what most modern people would say about the human situation—that is, until they think about it more carefully. He has been the most popular heresiarch of the modern age. If the reader doubts that, let him listen carefully to Pelagius's views in the historic debate on the nature of man and note the sympathy they evoke.[11]

[11] Direct quotations of Pelagius are taken from the excerpts of his writings found in *Documents of the Christian Church*, ed. Henry Bettenson (New York: Oxford University Press, 1947), pp. 74-75.

Pelagius was confident that man could do and could be what God required him to do and be. Indeed to question this proposition seemed to Pelagius to be questioning God's fairness and good sense.

We ascribe to the God of knowledge the guilt of twofold ignorance; ignorance of his own creation and of his own commands. As if, forgetting the weakness of men, his own creation, he had laid upon men commands which they were unable to bear. And at the same time (God forgive us!) we ascribe to the Just One unrighteousness, and cruelty to the Holy One; the first, by complaining that he has commanded the impossible, the second, by imagining that a man will be condemned by him for what he could not help; so that (the blasphemy of it!) God is thought of as seeking our punishment rather than our salvation. . . . No one knows the extent of our strength better than he who gave us that strength. . . . He has not willed to command anything impossible, for he is righteous; and he will not condemn a man for what he could not help, for he is holy.

Pelagius's preoccupation was moral self-discipline and reformation. As a popular teacher and preacher in Rome, he had drawn around him a group of followers attracted by the vigor of his demands for more seriousness and moral effort. From what we know of him, he sounds not unlike Dr. Frank Buchman in the twentieth century, who in his movement now known as Moral Re-armament has also appealed for a determined effort to lift the moral tone of individual and social life. Dr. Buchman proposed that men and women examine themselves against his demand for four moral qualities: absolute purity, absolute honesty, absolute love, and absolute sincerity. If anyone found himself falling short of the realization of these ideals, the remedy was simple: confess the shortcomings to a fellow-member of the Buchman Group and resolve not to fall short any more. This recommendation resembles the advice given to Charlie Brown in the cartoon strip "Peanuts" by the little girl who has set up as a psychiatrist (5¢ a visit): "Pull yourself together, 5¢ please." It presupposes the ability to do what one feels he must do. Christian orthodoxy sees that one can feel an obligation to do and be what he somehow never manages to do or be. To Pelagius this is nonsense; it is an evasion of responsibility. It means we have overestimated God's demands or underestimated our own strength —or both.

To the objection that Pelagius seems to have left God quite out of the picture, his reply was that we must ascribe to God the praise for having created us as free moral beings. He distinguished three factors in the moral act—the ability to act, the determination to act, and the moral action itself. God is responsible for the first, but man is responsible for the second and third. "Therefore man's praise lies in his willing and doing a good work; or rather this praise belongs both to man and to God who has granted the possibility of willing and working, and who by the help of his grace ever assists this very possibility." In that last phrase, Pelagius suggests that God inspires and encourages man's efforts, but it is made clear from the lines that precede it that determining to do good and actually performing it are almost altogether the result of man's own power—power which God has bestowed in his creation of man's freedom. "When we say that it is possible for a man to be without sin, we are even then praising God by acknowledging the gift of possibility which we have received." The role of God in the process of man's salvation is that of a friendly and enthusiastic coach, cheering the team on to victory, having trained and taught them all he can. He has given us the possibility of winning, but the decision to try as hard as we can and the actual skill and resourcefulness of the playing is fully our responsibility.

The negative side of Pelagius's teaching consists in denying that the fall of Adam has in any serious or crucial way crippled a man for the undertaking of the Christian life. So he wrote,

Everything good and everything evil, in respect of which we are either worthy of praise or of blame, is *done by us,* not *born with us.* We are not born in our full development, but with a capacity for good and evil; we are begotten as well without virtue as without vice.

St. Augustine summed up Pelagius's views (we cannot say exactly with what fairness or justice) in his *De Gestis Pelagii.*[12]

[12] Quoted in *Documents of the Christian Church,* p. 76.

i. Adam was created mortal and he would have died, whether he
sinned or not. ii. Adam's sin injured himself alone, not the human race.
iii. The Law, as well as the Gospel, leads to the Kingdom. iv. There
were men without sin before Christ's coming. v. Newborn infants are
in the same condition as Adam before the Fall.

Whether St. Augustine has been absolutely fair or not, the main
point seems clear: Pelagius believed man was free to respond to
the commandments and requirements of God, and he ought to be
encouraged to do so rather than excused for failing to do so by
some theory about original sin.

Choice and Freedom

For St. Augustine the Fall was catastrophic and,
therefore, man's problem was more desperate. He did not exactly
deny man's freedom. Everything man did he did by his own choice.
It was just that the range of his choices was limited, and he could
not choose to do all that he felt he ought to do. One might think of
a comparison in the example of a small child playing the piano. The
child can climb up on the piano stool and bang away happily,
choosing now to pound the white keys and now the black, and
everything the child does is done by his free choice. He can pound
away until he is bored and wanders off to find something else to do.
In this sense, he plays the piano quite freely. He is not free, however, to play "The Moonlight Sonata." There is a lack of capacity
and power which sets a limit to his freedom, even though within
that limit his acts are his own free choice. This is the state in which
man finds himself after the Fall, according to St. Augustine. His
struggles and his efforts are all the result of his free choice, but
they are all frustrated and limited by a lack of capacity which, until
it is supplied, dooms all his attempts to achieve goodness. Apart
from Christ, St. Augustine taught, all men are under "a cruel
necessity of sinning." Because of this, he must regard the whole
human race as, in his famous phrase, a "mass of perdition."

It has been observed that St. Augustine and Pelagius were really thinking of freedom in two very different—though not necessarily contradictory—ways. For Pelagius, freedom meant standing before a crossroads of decision and being able to go one way or the other. For St. Augustine, this kind of freedom seemed unimportant in contrast with another sort of freedom—the freedom to be and do what one most deeply wants to be and do. St. Augustine is not much concerned with the freedom of the child to pound the piano keys as long as he likes; he *is* concerned with the child's freedom to play great music. That latter sort of freedom can only be achieved at the price of limiting the unrestricted freedom of choice of which Pelagius talked. The love of great music means that one no longer has the freedom to play chopsticks—or at least that freedom has no importance and no meaning any more. When the power of great music captures the heart of a pianist, some of the possible theoretical choices about a piano—e.g., banging it haphazardly—are no longer live options. So St. Augustine believed that in the case of man he must exchange his bondage to sin not for unrestricted license but for the service and bondage to Christ which alone fulfills his best possibilities. In a famous passage, he contrasts three states of man with respect to freedom: Adam had the freedom to sin or not to sin; fallen man after Adam loses the freedom not to sin; Christ, the Second Adam, loses the freedom to sin! As St. Augustine saw it, sin had no more attraction to Christ than chopsticks has to a great pianist. It was not a live option. It was only theoretically a possibility for Christ.

Some of the questions raised in this historic debate must be postponed for another chapter, but the main points made by St. Augustine became the Christian orthodoxy about man in most areas of the Church.[13] In many ways he has been dramatically

---

[13] The major exception is the Eastern Orthodox churches, who took no part in the discussion and "have scarcely felt St. Augustine's influence at all." W. M. Horton, *Christian Theology, an Ecumenical Approach* (New York: Harper & Bros., 1955), p. 168. Cf. Professor Horton's description of modern questions urged against the Augustinian position and of the defense of it by Reinhold Niebuhr and others (*ibid.,* pp. 154-168).

vindicated by modern thinkers like Karl Marx and Sigmund Freud, both of whom tried to show how narrow and limited were the ranges of human freedom and how much men were captives of their class presuppositions and of their unconscious drives and impulses. These theories assume, as St. Augustine did, that freedom is not something man is born with but something he must be given in the processes of living. The naive liberalism of the eighteenth and nineteenth centuries had assumed that once the fetters of superstition, economic exploitation, political tyranny, and ecclesiastical dogmatism could be broken man would automatically find and enjoy his freedom. The loneliness and fretfulness of modern life have shown how false that assumption is, and the rise of Naziism and Communism in which modern men, indeed often times the most emancipated in the old liberal sense of the word, gladly renounce their freedom of choice and accept the bondage of an implausible and preposterous creed in order to find meaning for their lives, has been a sobering lesson for the Pelagian heretics of our time. The power of false religions like the Hitler and Marxist creeds is proof of the necessity for religious commitment if man is to fulfill himself, and yet where can man find a commitment that is not itself so shot through with human presumption and self-centredness that like the Nazi and Communist faiths they destroy those who serve them? Until men see this question as an urgent and inescapable one, they will not comprehend the promise and the offer of the Christian Gospel.

Is Original Sin a "Moral Hypochondria"?

There is a general impression that, whether true or not, the doctrine of original sin had better not be emphasized too much since its main effect is a depressing and defeatist one. Professor Charles Frankel, in his book *The Case for Modern Man,* argues that the doctrine represents "moral hypochondria" and that it gives no guidance to man at all in the practical living out of his life because it condemns all human activities indiscriminately as sin and that's an end to it.[14] Professor Frankel is correct in his understanding of the doctrine of sin as one which brings all human activities under the judgment of God and condemns them all. The same point is made in an anonymous jingle composed at the time of the famous Gifford Lectures of Reinhold Niebuhr in 1939:

> Of the lecture when Niebuhr had quit it,
> A bright student said, "Ah, I've hit it.
> Since I cannot do right,
> On this very night
> I'll choose some sin to commit and commit it!"

The point of the limerick, however, is the fact that the choice of which particular sin to commit is not at all an unimportant one. All we think and do and say bears marks of our disorganized personalities, but this does not lead a Christian to paralysis of effort, as we shall have occasion to see more fully in a later chapter. To decide what action to take is part of man's functional as a rational and self-conscious being, and he cannot abrogate it, even though the doctrine of sin suggests the hindrances and limitations under which he has to work.

The doctrine of original sin does not all by itself determine man's decisions, but it does set them in a context of modesty and compassion and tolerance. It checks man's perennial temptation to cast all his judgments in the form of black or white, absolutely good or absolutely evil. It opens a man's ears and eyes to what others say and enables him to sympathize with them more fully. Professor Herbert Butterfield has observed that the whole tradition of diplomatic negotiations between states rests on an assumption that no one state is ever wholly right or wholly wrong.[15] Self-confessed sinners meet one another in an atmosphere of mutual suspicion but

[14] Cf. C. Frankel, *The Case for Modern Man* (New York: Harper & Bros., 1956), the chapter "The Rediscovery of Sin," pp. 85-116.

[15] Cf. *Christianity, Diplomacy and War* (New York: Abingdon-Cokesbury, 1953). "In time of war we should expect the Christian to have compassion somewhere even for the enemy, and even for the wicked—expect him also to be diffident about believing that his own nation's cause is absolutely the righteous one, and all the wickedness on the side of the enemy." (p. 5).

of mutual sympathy and understanding as well. "He is a sinner—but then, so am I." So the doctrine of human sin draws out of human conflicts and controversies the sting of ferocity and vindictiveness. By locating the center of the human problem in the self-assertiveness and imperialism of the human heart, the doctrine of original sin makes a man modest about all human programs—even his own—and sensitizes his conscience to the lingering elements of willfulness and prejudice in his best judgments and most altruistic actions. It is not "hypochondria" to recognize the power of a disease which is actually disabling and crippling in its effects. It is, on the contrary, a mark of realism and an indispensable prerequisite for seeking healing and salvation.

Hypocrisy and Pessimism

The Christian orthodoxy about man helps to explain the prevalence of hypocrisy in human actions. Hypocrisy is only possible because man is a sinner but not so lost in his sin that he does not want to rise above it. If a man were such a sinner that he didn't care, then he would never go to the trouble of fabricating the hypocritical self-defense which enables him to accept himself more fully. The fact that men are not able to violate the standards of ethics by which they live without finding some extenuating circumstances to justify it or some plausible disguise by which to misrepresent it is an important testimony both to man's dignity and to his fallen condition. If man were better than he is, he would never have to stoop to such hypocrisy—but if he were worse than he is, he would never stoop to it either! In other words, hypocrisy is what one would expect from a being made in the image of God and yet living consistently for himself. Hypocrisy is a sign of hope in human nature, for it represents that residual moral sensitivity—perverted and twisted as it is—which proves that a man can still be appealed to and still be reached by the purposes of love and faith.

What shall we say to those who complain that there is enough pessimism about man abroad in the world already and that we scarcely need Christianity's gloomy orthodoxy to add to the chorus of woe and frustration? Isn't the doctrine of original sin just what Professor Frankel calls it—"moral hypochondria"? That charge might be valid if men were asked to look only at themselves, preoccupied with their own symptoms and bewailing their own deficiencies. But the sense of sin in the Bible is not the result of a preoccupation with one's self. It is the result of a vision of the being and beauty and holiness and love of God himself. Only when man's life is measured against that standard does the full implication of his tragedy become clear. For the Christian the first thing the coming of Christ into human life does for us is to deepen our sense of sin. Here is what we might be; consider in his light the tragedy of what we are. But the moment we see him as the embodiment of moral demands which we can never meet, we also see him as the embodiment of a new possibility for our lives, as the guarantor of divine forgiveness and initiator of a whole new orientation toward life, as the source of new power and new meaning for our existence. The diagnosis of sin and the offer of health and salvation are inextricably intertwined in Christianity. One cannot be understood apart from the other. It is the same Christ who is the standard by which we are condemned and the Saviour in whom we find new hope and new strength. If Christianity goes further than any other great religion in the demands it makes upon men it is because it goes further than any other religion in the offer it makes to men. One of the reasons why Judaism has never followed Christianity— after an initial attempt to do so—in its doctrine of original sin is that it has lacked the central figure of Jesus the Christ. From him Christianity gains the insight by which men can be more deeply and seriously judged but also the power to accept that judgment without despair.

The Dualism of Marcion

Because Christianity's offer means nothing apart from Christianity's demand, the Church early rejected the heresy of

Marcion which sought to separate the two and put them in opposition to one another. For Marcion there were virtually two gods—one the god of law and demand, whose judgments were unbearable and whose face therefore was one of wrath, and the other the god of love and grace, whose only message was forgiveness, and whose face therefore was one of pity. Marcion believed the first god must be superseded by the second. Christianity rejected any such dualism at the heart of reality. Wrath and love are not two gods. They are two ways in which the One God of the Bible appears to a man as he is either a rebellious sinner or a grateful obedient son. God's love —like the love of serious and conscientious parents—is not just indulgence but a fierce determination that the beloved shall become all that his possibilities and capacities suggest. Any one who was blessed with good parents knows that there is no dualism between love and wrath. The same parent will manifest one or the other depending on the child's attitude and orientation. If the child insists on missing his opportunities and spoiling his possibilities, he will know parental wrath. If he seeks to realize his possibilities and fulfill his capacities, he will know parental love and approval. The explanation of God's wrath is the doctrine of sin. It is the other side of his holy love—the side which rebellious and wayward man sees until he comes to a change of heart. The Old Testament and the New Testament reveal one God, and although the Old Testament may lay stress on his demands and his law it also has much to say about his forgiveness and his love. The New Testament—as even the most casual reading will show—does not leave behind the idea of divine wrath even though its major attention may be said to be on the grace and forgiveness of God in Jesus Christ.

This paradox of divine wrath and divine love is reproduced in the human experience of sin and grace. The more the Christian comes to know God in Christ and to live in his presence and by his power, the more deeply he sees the reality of his own sin and the more dependent he becomes upon God's mercy and acceptance. Yet the very knowledge of the depths of that mercy makes the sin even more heinous. So once again as in other areas of Christian thought, orthodoxy about man is paradoxical, many-sided, holding together in the same way they are found together in experience itself contrasting yet complementary understandings of the human situation. As we come to the end of our discussion of man and his condition we have already begun to talk about the source of his health and salvation, because apart from Christ we could never face ourselves so frankly. This is not hypochondria but the sanest and deepest analysis of the problem of being a man that the world has ever known, and because it goes so deep it plumbs the heart of men and corresponds to longings and yearnings which apart from Christ would seem wildly improbable. To the same Christ by whom we measure our fallen condition we now turn for new status and new dignity and new power.

CHAPTER SIX

Jesus Christ,
Come in the Flesh

THE major task of Christian orthodoxy, beside which all other responsibilities are secondary and peripheral, is to understand aright the person and work of Jesus Christ. Christianity is unique among the religions of the world, of course, by reason of his role in its piety, devotion, and life; and consequently it is not surprising that the Church has expended such a prodigious amount of intellectual energy in achieving a satisfactory expression of what Christians believe about him. Controversies in this area of Christian thought have produced a vehemence and a passion which testify to how central and crucial these questions have been. Even in the New Testament itself the intensity of the discussion begins to show itself in the heated language employed. "Who is the liar but he who denies that Jesus is the Christ?" (I John 2:22). Legend has it that in the controversies of the fourth century about the relationship of Jesus Christ to the Father rival gangs of stevedores, singing lusty theological jingles, clashed with each other on the docks of Alexandria over the issue! Whatever prejudices the reader may have about the ivory-tower character of theological dis-

cussion, here at least in the doctrines about Jesus Christ grass-roots
Christians have felt their deepest experiences and convictions to
be at stake and have responded with appropriate passion and
energy. In its early days Christianity was in many ways a flexible
and adaptable religion, but when any question was raised which
seemed to impugn the status and uniqueness of Jesus Christ, there
was manifest at once a rock-ribbed stubbornness which not even
the threats of banishment, torture, and death could move. Nowhere
else in the whole realm of theological thought does the dogmatic
spirit flame so brightly as in this central question of the Christian
religion: who is Jesus Christ and what is the meaning of his life
and death and resurrection?

The discussion which follows will lead the reader along the
rather tortuous paths of the prolonged Christological controversies
of the fourth and fifth centuries. The distinctions will often seem
excessively technical and even picayune, perhaps. Behind all the
debates, however, lay this great question, and the modern Christian
will do well to keep it in mind as he tries to assess the usefulness of
the traditional formulae about Christ for modern thought: how
does this understanding of Jesus Christ touch the problem of my
anxiety and pride and self-centredness? As we shall see later, this
question was the one which most concerned the great Athanasius,
who led the forces of orthodoxy in the fourth century against the
recurrent popularity of the teachings of Arius. Athanasius was not
so much interested in the logical precision and consistency of his
position as a philosophical proposition. In these respects his teaching can be criticized, and in Arius's letters we catch the tone of
condescension of a trained philosophical mind for the amateurish
efforts of his opponents. But the amateurs grasped firmly one principle which Arius himself never fully appreciated, and that was that
the crucial question about the doctrine of Christ was not whether
it could be made neat and consistent but whether it expressed the
overwhelming experience of Christian salvation. What kind of a
Christ can save man from his predicament? It is this kind of a
Christ that we have met and known and worshipped. It is he who
convinces us that life at its heart and source is trustworthy. It is he

who assures us that God forgives and accepts us as his sons without regard for all our failures and inadequacies. It is he who quickens our love and devotion and so supplies the new motive power for living the good life. It is he who provides us with the ultimate measurement of responsibility and forbearance toward our fellow-men and introduces into every human relationship a boundless generosity which saves human society from disintegration and fratricide. Only when we have tried to catalogue all that Christ does for human life, are we ready to decide how to express our convictions about him most adequately and accurately. The doctrine of Christ grows out of the Christian's religious experience and must always be tested against it and judged in the light of it. "Who on earth can set me free from the clutches of my own sinful nature?" asks St. Paul, and it is in answer to this question that he develops his conviction about "Jesus Christ our Lord." [1]

The Doctrine of Christ

A glance at the New Testament, even of the most cursory sort, will show how this development began at the very outset of the Christian movement. The impact Jesus Christ made on the Christian community was quite unlike that made by any other figure in the long history of the Jewish religious tradition. Even the towering giants—Abraham, Moses, David, Elijah—had no such revolutionary significance for their contemporaries as he had. It is inconceivable to suppose Moses saying: "I am the way, the truth, and the life," or to imagine Elijah promising, "Come unto me, all ye that travail and are heavy laden, and I will refresh you." The natural and unostentatious way in which the figure of Jesus Christ is put at the center of the New Testament, to a degree that is unique in all Jewish religious literature, is a sign of the centrality of his role in Christian experience. He makes claims and promises, he receives devotion and homage, he deliberately draws

[1] Romans 7:24-25 in the translation by J. B. Phillips, *Letters to Young Churches* (New York: Macmillan, 1948), p. 16.

men to himself—all in such a way as to suggest that he has a right to the place in men's hearts and lives which is usually reserved for God. When in the book of the Acts of the Apostles Stephen is about to be martyred, his prayer is a natural one for any Christian to make—but an astonishing prayer for any non-Christian Jew and one which is for Jewish orthodoxy a species of blasphemy—"Lord Jesus, receive my spirit." To people who pray like that the question of who is Jesus Christ is no mere theological conundrum; it is the most urgent question they have ever asked or answered.

An impact like this is only explicable on the assumption that an historical person was responsible for it. In the first muscle-flexing of New Testament criticism in the nineteenth century it was fashionable to prove how emancipated scholars could be by setting out to deny that an historical person, Jesus of Nazareth, ever existed at all. That effort, ingenious and imaginative as it was and proof of the endless probing and questioning capacity of the inquiring mind, must nevertheless be judged a failure. The fact of the Christian Church and of its literature in the New Testament can have no other convincing explanation but the existence of an historical person, identifiable as Jesus of Nazareth. It would be as easy to imagine Naziism without the figure of Adolf Hitler or Indian nationalism without the figure of Mahatma Gandhi as to imagine the Christian Church of the first century without the historical figure of Jesus Christ. No other theory of Christian origins has yet appeared which accounts for the facts as readily and naturally as the assumption that there appeared during the reign of Tiberias Caesar in the provinces of Judea and Galilee a person named Jesus, who was put to death and yet appeared to his followers after three days to be unmistakably and fully alive, and was subsequently revered as their Lord and their God.

Jesus, Son of God

To make this historical judgment, however, in no way proves that the Christian Church's interpretation and understanding of Jesus was the correct one. This interpretation and understanding are implied on every page of the New Testament and at some points are baldly stated. "The gospel of Jesus Christ, the Son of God" declares the Gospel according to St. Mark, a document which most scholars believe is in its present form one of the oldest of the accounts of Jesus' life, death, and resurrection. This prefatory announcement warns the reader that here is no unbiased, scientifically dispassionate, objective account of an interesting figure in human history, but rather a devout and faithful rendering of the meaning of One who is believed to be the unique Son of God himself. This Christian bias is the only excuse that Christians had for recording the story at all. It is well known that no contemporary non-Christian historian or biographer thought Jesus of Nazareth a sufficiently important figure to deserve literary attention at all. All we know about Jesus we know as a result of literature which is hopelessly prejudiced from the outset by its conviction that in him men were dealing with God himself. Attempts to distill from the Gospel account an historically accurate—because theologically neutral—picture of Jesus, one which would correspond to a talking motion picture of his life and actions, is now widely regarded as virtually impossible. The significance of Jesus Christ for human life is not a question that can be proved by historical investigation. All the conclusions which a solid and scientific historical study of the New Testament can yield have their importance, for they make clearer and more precise just what it is that the early Church believed about Jesus Christ. But the final question of whether their estimate of him was correct is decided only by the faith-decision of the questioner himself.

If one does not share the Christian Church's understanding of the significance of Jesus Christ, then it is hard to see what else one can make of him from the documents which are extant about him. Efforts to depict him as a gentle and kindly teacher of ethics, morality, and religion run head on into the fact that the Gospel records support no such picture at all. A modest and skillful teacher, for example, would seek to minimize more and more his own significance and free his students more and more from any sort of dependence upon him. Jesus in the Gospels does exactly the opposite. As the Gospel stories proceed (we speak here primarily of the three Synoptic Gospels, since the Gospel of St. John does not record this kind of development) Jesus speaks more and more of himself, his own role as Messiah, the importance of loyalty and faith and remembrance of him. Rather than lead his students to dispense with his services, Jesus draws and binds them more closely to himself, as if indeed he were himself the Truth rather than just a teacher of it. Marxist attempts to portray Jesus as a social reformer are even less credible, for all his recorded sayings reveal a disinclination for such a role and an uncompromising idealism that is very unsuitable for specific guidance in questions of social reform. It may, of course, be true that the Christian Church has distorted and misrepresented the historic Jesus almost beyond recognition, but if so, the damage was done nearly 2,000 years ago and any attempt to undo it labors under impossible difficulties, and is usually more ingenious than convincing. Unless Jesus was what the Church thought he was—the only-begotten Son of God—then he had best be forgotten and ignored, because we have all been the victims of a gigantic hoax.

Demythologizing

One of the lively discussions of contemporary theology concerning Jesus Christ and the New Testament record of him revolves around the name of the German scholar, Rudolf Bultmann. His main purpose has been to penetrate behind the myths in which, he points out, the New Testament accounts are enshrined —myths which speak of angels, a three-storied universe, miraculous events, risings from the dead, etc.—to discover the "understanding of existence" which is there enshrined.[2] Thus the Crucifixion and Resurrection are not just "an event of the past which can be con-

[2] Quotations are from *Kerygma and Myth,* ed. by H. W. Bartsch (London: SPCK, 1953), which contains a discussion between Bultmann and some of his critics.

templated in detachment" but something which challenges and grips modern man and demands from him an appropriate response. Bultmann describes the significance of the Cross, for example, as follows: "The overcoming of our natural dread of suffering and the perfection of our detachment from the world." [3] Or again Bultmann says, "Cross and resurrection form a single, indivisible cosmic event which brings judgment to the world and opens up for men the possibility of authentic life." [4] This is the way to think about Jesus Christ and the events concerning him which the Gospels record.

Indeed, Bultmann says that the New Testament itself seeks to be understood in this personal, existential way. Our question should not be: Did this happen exactly as it is recorded? Rather our question should be: What is God saying to me and seeking to achieve in me through my hearing of this story? The late Bishop Nicolai of Serbia made the same point in a story of his imprisonment in Dachau by the Nazis during World War II. He was derided by the guard for reading his Bible so diligently. "Don't you know," said the guard, "that our German critics have destroyed the value of that book?" "This book," the bishop replied, "was not given that we might criticize it, but that it might criticize *us*." Bultmann would apparently agree that this is the legitimate answer of Christian piety to critical New Testament scholarship.

Has Historicity Any Importance?

One would want to ask, however, whether this means that the question of historicity has *no* importance whatever for faith.[5] Is the story about Jesus Christ to be regarded like the story of Prometheus, a challenging and stirring account the factual na-

[3] *Ibid.,* p. 37.
[4] *Ibid.,* p. 39.
[5] In fairness to Professor Bultmann it must be said that he does not deny or question the historical character of the Cross. Cf. *Ibid.,* p. 110: "I do not mean that it is timeless like an abstract idea, for that would make the cross a bare symbol. I am seeking rather to give full weight to the New Testament conception of the cross as an ever-present reality."

ture of which is altogether irrelevant for its usefulness and power as a myth which helps to interpret the meaning of human existence? Isn't is true that, unlike the myth of Prometheus, the story of Jesus Christ is deliberately by the Gospel writers given an historical setting? "In the fifteenth year of the reign of Tiberius Caesar" says the evangelist much as if someone were to preface a story today with the time-note, "In the first administration of Dwight Eisenhower." The power of the story of Jesus Christ is not independent of its having happened historically, as Bultmann himself seems ready to acknowledge. It may be spiritually unhealthy to ask for too much historical detail where historical detail can no longer be supplied, but historical fact is never irrelevant to Christian faith. The fact that God came into history means that he puts himself at the disposal of man's historical inquiries, and exactly what he did and said obviously make a great difference to Christian faith. If we can with confidence know nothing at all about the historical Jesus, then the Christian faith is reduced to an assertion that a kind of mysterious Mr. X, whose character and conduct are virtually blank to us, died and was supposed by his disciples to rise again from the dead. Even on Professor Bultmann's own terms, that is not a very powerful or moving story. The power of the Gospel lies in the fact that precisely such a person as Jesus is shown to be in the Gospel accounts—one who spoke as he spoke and did what he did—underwent the crucifixion and resurrection experiences and is declared to be the Son of God as a consequence. The processes of historical investigation help to determine more accurately what he said and what he did. Insofar as this process is successful—and we must be as modest about it as its findings require—it ministers to Christian faith and generates new power and assurance about the Gospel itself. It is tempting amidst the uncertainties generated by modern biblical criticism to take the extreme position that no matter what the critics decide my Christian faith is shaken not at all, but this is too sweeping to be consistent with Christian orthodoxy. It amounts to saying that the historical character of Christianity is not significant for faith, and this is an ancient heresy combatted even in the New Testament itself again and again.

Docetism

One way this heresy was expressed was in what we usually call Docetism, from the Greek word *dokeo,* which means "to appear." This heresy would claim that Jesus only appeared to be an historical, physical, human person and that he was in reality a kind of ghost-like being, whose teachings are valuable quite apart from his own historical existence. The New Testament writers, especially the author of the Epistles of John and the Gospel according to John, make strenuous efforts to oppose this heresy. The opening words of the first epistle of John strike an almost crude note in the effort to emphasize the physicality and historicity of Jesus Christ. "We are writing to you about something which has always existed yet which we ourselves actually saw and heard: something which we have had opportunity to observe closely and even to hold in our hands, and yet, as we know now, was something of the very Word of Life himself." [6] Apparently the New Testament Christians were not dismissing as irrelevant the question of the physical and historical existence of Jesus Christ. He must be, as the epistle of John puts it in another place, "Jesus Christ, come in the flesh."

Why is this? Why can we not take Jesus' words and Jesus' story the same way in which we take the myth of Prometheus? The answer lies in the nature of the Christian experience of redemption and salvation. The Christian Gospel is a proclamation of an event —not the appearance of a new idea. This event has mighty and incalculable implications, but if it never happened, then the implications would not be anything to bother about. Precisely because "the very Word of Life himself" could be "observed closely" and "held in our hands," the Christian Gospel transforms man's whole estimate of himself, his world, his destiny, his God. To compare various world religions as to the quality of their teachings is to miss precisely the point about Christianity. It is not about teachings; it

---

[6] I John 1:1, in the translation by J. B. Phillips, *Letters to Young Churches* (New York: Macmillan, 1948), p. 209.

is about an event in history. Something happened. God became the subject of human experience and lived the life of humanity. The Christians of the New Testament had been grasped and turned completely around and born all over again because they accepted this event and let it have its way with them. If Jesus Christ had only appeared to be a man, then the whole power of the Gospel was lost. The Sermon on the Mount and the Lord's Prayer and the parables of the Prodigal Son and the Good Samaritan must be consigned to the catalogue of inspiring and visionary religious idealism, no more and no less important than similar material found elsewhere in world religious literature. But what if Christianity were right? What if this person was indeed God himself come in the flesh? What if the Sermon on the Mount was an expression in words of what was actually lived out in the flesh? What if the parables were not just fanciful dreams of what life might be like but stories of what God himself was doing for men in the person of Jesus Christ? It was the conviction of the Christian Church that all this was indeed true, and they passionately rejected any suggestion of the heresy of Docetism, because it undermined the whole Christian experience and destroyed the exhilarating assurance by which they lived.

The Word of God

Somewhat later another conviction about the nature of Jesus Christ had to be clarified and nailed down in unmistakable language. What is meant by saying that he is the only-begotten Son of God, the Word of God, the image of the invisible God? The language of the New Testament on this point is vague and unspecific. Leonard Hodgson has said that the New Testament Christians were religious Trinitarians but theological Unitarians. That is to say, their way of speaking about Jesus Christ had not yet quite caught up with their religious experience of him. That is true also of many modern Christians who hesitate to speak of Jesus as divine and yet refer to him as Master and Lord, which if the words are taken seriously implies a status which is nothing less than divine. For who has the right to absolute mastery or lordship over a man's life except God? If Jesus is the absolute sovereign over my life then for all practical purposes he is God, no matter how I may balk at using the word. The developed confession of faith in the Christian Church about Jesus Christ only comes when men reflect and think out the implications of their deepest Christian experience. As we shall see presently, the Christian experience of salvation through Christ led inevitably to the confession of the orthodox creeds that he is "Very God of very God . . . of one substance with the Father."

An early attempt within the New Testament period itself to picture the relationship of Jesus Christ to God the Father was made by the Gospel according to St. John. Here the evangelist borrowed an idea that had already been used to bring together Jewish and Greek ways of thinking by the interesting Hellenized Jew, Philo, who was a contemporary of our Lord's. Philo had seized upon the Stoic idea of "The Word" and used it to interpret many Old Testament passages where God is depicted as addressing Wisdom or Spirit. For the Stoics "The Word" is God's great idea about the world, about its structure and laws and purpose. It is the divine model on which the whole of reality is planned. This Word is not, however, inert and lifeless, but an active and energetic agent, working in nature and within the hearts and minds of men to form and shape life according to God's purpose. Just as the word of an author takes shape within a book and then is sent out to the public to influence their thinking and to shape their opinions, so the Word of God becomes a kind of secondary divinity, mediating the divine purpose to men.[7]

St. John's Gospel thinks of Christ as fulfilling this same func-

[7] Cf. this passage of Philo's, quoted in C. K. Barrett, *The New Testament Background: Selected Documents* (London: S.P.C.K., 1958), p. 184: "To his Word, his chief messenger, highest in age and honour, the Father of all has given the special prerogative, to stand on the border and separate the creature from the Creator. This same Word both pleads with the immortal as suppliant for afflicted mortality and acts as ambassador of the ruler to the subject."

tion. The Prologue of the Gospel says, in effect, that God has from the very outset been sending out his great Idea into the world. This Idea has been planted within the heart and mind of every man that is born into the world, but despite this fact men have rejected and resisted it. In Jesus Christ, however, this Idea has come in a new and compelling and decisive way. It has become flesh and has dwelt among us. So, St. John is saying, Jesus Christ is as closely and as intimately related to God the Father as an idea is close to the man who conceives it. "The Word was with God, and the Word was God."

This insistence that the origin of Jesus Christ must be sought in the eternal mind and purpose of God himself was not everywhere accepted, at least not quite as St. John's Gospel seems to picture it. There was a party in the early Church who were called the "Alogi," which means those who would not use the Logos or Word as a title for Jesus Christ. They seem to have believed that he was just an inspired human being, different only in degree from Moses and the prophets and saints of Judaism.[8] Some support for this point of view was thought to be found in St. Mark's Gospel where the coming of the Holy Spirit upon Jesus in the Baptism is immediately followed by the divine declaration: "Thou art my beloved Son, in whom I am well pleased." This point of view was sometimes called Adoptionism and is specifically attacked by Irenaeus, the second-century Church Father, who speaks of one such teacher who held that Jesus was not born of the Holy Ghost of the Virgin Mary but was the son of Mary and Joseph "like other men, but superior to all others in justice, prudence, and wisdom." [9] The shortcoming of this approach to the question of

---

[8] Although not technically a member of the Alogi, the third-century heretic, Paul of Samosata, held some such view apparently, and is quoted as saying of the birth from Mary, "What she bore was a man equal to us, but superior in all things as a result of holy spirit." Quoted in J. N. D. Kelley, *Early Christian Doctrines* (New York: Harper & Bros., 1958), p. 140.

[9] Quoted from H. Bettenson, *op. cit.*, p. 52. Notice that Irenaeus sees the doctrine of the virginal conception of Jesus as a way of safeguarding His uniquely divine origin. Since St. John's Gospel safeguards this idea in another way, he does not think it important to recount the story of the virgin birth at all.

the nature of Jesus Christ, as Christian orthodoxy came to see, was that it did not put the emphasis sufficiently strongly on God's initiative and personal involvement in the being of Christ. Jesus Christ is not just a man whom God inspired. If that is the substance of the Christian faith, it does not at all answer the anxiety of the human heart nor the problem of the attitude of God toward man's rebellion and self-centredness. The origins of Jesus Christ must lie deep within the eternal being and purpose of God himself, and it must be God himself who is personally involved in the life and experience of Jesus Christ.

The Arian Controversy

This last requirement of Christian orthodoxy came to be insisted upon in the famous Arian controversy of the fourth century. Although he accepted wholeheartedly the Johannine use of the Logos as a way of conceiving the relationship of Christ to the Father, Arius, who was a sophisticated and brilliant—if somewhat self-satisfied—theological teacher of Alexandria, expounded the Logos idea in a way that revealed one of its fatal inadequacies. For Arius the Word was created and sent forth by God, but there was an important line and distinction drawn between the two. The Word was not—like God himself—eternal and unbegotten. So Arius writes plainly to his friend Eusebius, Bishop of Nicomedia, "And before he was begotten or created or appointed or established [Arius is not particular which word one uses to express the fact that the Son was brought into being] he did not exist; for he was not unbegotten. We are persecuted because we say that the Son has a beginning, but God is without beginning." [10] Here is the essence of what the Council of Nicea was to decide was an heretical understanding of the nature of the Son of God. He must be distinguished, Arius urged, from the Father, who alone was eternal and unbegotten. If one were to draw a line between the Creator and all that he has created, the Son would be on the cre-

[10] Quoted in Bettenson, *op. cit.*, p. 55.

ated side of the line. Arius did not, of course, say that the Son of God was only a man. He was the first of all the created things and through him all other things came to be. He was a kind of superangel, and all the honor and reverence and devotion which the Church paid to him was richly deserved. But when it came down to the precise definition of Deity, he could not be called God, for he was not eternal but had a beginning.

The Defense of Athanasius

Arius's famous opponent, Athanasius, took up the struggle against this position, for it seemed to him that the whole Christian experience and tradition was at stake. There could be no quibbling and no compromise; either Arius was wrong or Christianity was a fraud and idolatrous. It was a fraud, because in Arius's view God had not *come* in Christ but had simply *sent* Christ as His messenger and representative. God's love could only be proved if he was himself involved personally in the Incarnation. A well-meaning gesture of sending a personal representative would not, as Athanasius saw it, serve as an adequate substitute. What is more, Athanasius argued, if Arius is right then Christianity is idolatrous, for it encourages and promotes the worship of one who is not really God. If our thanks and praise are addressed to Christ and Christ is only a created being—albeit the highest and most important of all created beings—then Christians worship one who is less than God, and that is the definition of idolatry. To save the Christian religion and the Christian assurance of salvation Athanasius felt obliged to set up a test phrase which would screen out any Arian understanding of St. John's logos idea. The test phrase was a Greek word which we translate into English as "of one substance with the Father." That is to say, Athanasius wanted to say that Christ was in every respect fully God, eternal, uncreated, personally identical with God the Father. The controversy waxed long and fierce. At times it seemed as if Athanasius could not possibly prevail, and the phrase was coined *Athanasius contra mundum* (Athanasius against the whole world).[11] It must be supposed that the final triumph of the Nicene orthodoxy was due to the dawning realization that nothing less than the whole Christian faith was at stake.

Human *vs.* Divine

The real difficulty in dealing with modern heresies which deny the deity of Christ is that for the most part they do not begin with the fundamental Christian experience of salvation through Christ in the orthodox sense of that term. If the human problem is, as many moderns still suppose, only a problem of firing the human will and illuminating the human mind, then, of course, a superior and eloquent human being, given to saying quotable and inspiring things will do very well. Since we have known of several other such human beings in history, it seems best just to add Jesus Christ to the list and skip all the word-twisting, brain-torturing arguments about Deity, humanity, and all the rest. The New Testament is unanimous, however, in analyzing the human situation as much more desperate than just a problem of inspiration and illumination. As we have already seen, the human problem is a tragic and radical loss of power and capacity to become what we want and ought to be. Only a power which can grip and possess and transform us completely and totally will meet the depths of the human problem. The New Testament knew that only God could rightfully exercise such power in the human heart; indeed only God has such power to wield. Inspiring and eloquent teachers leave untouched the fundamental problem of man's distrust of life itself, of his persistent suspicion that he must make his own way and carve out his own destiny in a hostile and indifferent universe, and of the gnawing realization that he is not

[11] Among the arguments against the use of the phrase "of the same substance" was that it was non-scriptural, controversial and had never before been known in the Church. But here, as oftentimes, orthodoxy and traditional usage are not at all the same thing.

adequate for the task. The teaching of Judaism—that behind that universe is a holy God who demands self-forgetful love as a condition for fulfillment of life—only deepens man's desperation and increases his frantic self-assertion. Men who measure the human tragedy in this profound way hear the words of Jesus: "Come unto me, all ye that travail and are heavy laden, and I will refresh you." Only if those words come from the heart and mind of God himself do they begin to reach the human problem and to deal with it. As *human* consolation they are well-meaning, but pompous and ineffective. Only as the *divine* offer of new status and new fellowship and new power do these words make possible the new relationship of trust and of hope and of love. All this was at stake as Christians came to insist upon creedal language, which would make unmistakably clear the full deity of Christ. "God of God, Light of Light, Very God of very God, Being of one substance with the Father, By whom all things were made." Only a Christ who can appropriately be addressed like that can be the Lord and Saviour of the Christian faith.

The Apollinarian Heresy

The growing agreement, however, that Christ must be reverenced as fully God led to controversies in another crucial area of thought. In what sense can we say that he is human? A vigorous defender of the Nicene orthodoxy, like Apollinarius, stern opponent of Arianism that he was, strayed outside the limits of orthodoxy in the opposite direction and seems to have asserted that in Christ the divine Word took the place of the human soul or mind so that the Incarnate Christ was not fully and wholly man.[12] This the Church rejected decisively, although not all subsequent Christian piety has been as unequivocal. In modern times

[12] Scholars have questioned whether this statement of Apollinarianism really represents his views, since we must reconstruct his position from nothing more than isolated fragments of his writings. Whether or not Apollinarius was an Apollinarian, this commonly accepted version of his teachings must be adjudged heretical.

the discovery of the extent to which Jesus spoke and thought in the idiom, and with the limitations, of his own time has shocked and disturbed Christians who were in effect Apollinarian in their view of Christ. How dare scholars and biblical critics say that Jesus was mistaken in any matter? The passages where he is quoted in the Gospels as having predicted the catastrophic end of history within the lifetime of his hearers represent either misunderstandings or misquotations of what he really said. But this robs the Lord of his full human qualities. It means that although omniscient and foreseeing all things fully and completely, he nevertheless moved condescendingly among men, feigning an ignorance and emotions he did not fully experience, playing at being a man. As we shall see later, such a view of Christ's nature is fatal for any appreciation of his work. Apollinarianism produces a false Christ, practicing a profound deception upon gullible followers. He must as a man enter fully into time and space and participate fully in finite existence if the Incarnation is to be real at all.

The real issue in the Apollinarian heresy is the redeemability of man's whole nature. Can the very center of man's personality be rescued and transformed or must we assume that only by replacing this center with the Divine Personality can the union of human and divine be effected? Once having asserted the full deity of Christ the Church began a battle against a persistent reluctance to accord him a full humanity, a reluctance apparently based upon a suspicion of man as a finite personal being. Somehow, these opponents thought, his human nature must be radically and seriously qualified before it can be thought fit for union with godhead. Surely this is too deep a pessimism about man. This asserts, in effect, that the gulf between human and divine, between finite and infinite, can never be bridged at all except on terms that virtually eliminate and annihilate the human and the finite. Gregory of Nyssa saw the issue clearly when he wrote, "What he has not assumed he has not healed." With Apollinarianism the Church began a long and tortuous controversy—one which is in many ways not yet fully resolved—over the full human personality of Jesus

Christ. In one way and then another the heresy of Apollinarianism appeared and reappeared. The history of theological controversy for the next hundred and twenty-five years after Nicaea—and longer—was the history of a reluctant church, inhibited by the Greek philosophical depreciation of the finite, material, human realm, being forced by the inner logic of the Christian experience to acknowledge a full and genuine human personality in Jesus Christ.

The Nestorian Thesis

The controversy can only be inadequately summarized here. Once it was decided at the Ecumenical Council of Constantinople in 351 that Apollinarianism would not do and that it must be affirmed that Christ took unto himself a full human nature—soul and mind as well as body and flesh—then the controversy took a new form. How were human and divine united? The suggestion of Nestorius, the Archbishop of Constantinople, whatever its deficiencies had at least the advantage of acknowledging a full and perfect human personality in Christ. He insisted on this to such an extent and made such a sharp distinction between human and divine[13] that his problem was how to account for and express the *union* between the two. He used the text about marriage between husband and wife: "The twain shall become one flesh." "Here is how human and divine are related in Christ," said Nestorius in effect. "It is like the cooperative harmony developed between a man and his wife. It is a union of wills and personalities, wondrously full and complete, once effected and never destroyed."

[13] Nestorius underlined this sharp distinction by his refusal to accord the title "God-bearer" or "Mother of God" (*theotokos* in Greek) to St. Mary. "She is the mother of the human Jesus," he argued, "but how can she be called the Mother of God without blasphemy and absurdity?" The orthodox answer was that the union of human and divine had resulted in a single person, and since she was the Mother of that single human-divine person she could properly be addressed as Mother of God.

It might be objected facetiously that Nestorius appears not to have had much experience as a marriage counselor, for the choice of the marital union as a symbol and analogue of the Incarnation reflects a very optimistic view of matrimony. The objection of his opponents was that such a union seemed merely external and accidental and that it suggested a personality which, in our modern psychological jargon, we should call schizophrenic. It just may be, of course, that Nestorius was the forerunner without quite knowing it of the present-day theologians of personal relationship and that his analogy between marriage and the Incarnation is truer to our own understanding of the ways of God in human hearts than the outmoded metaphysical language of his opponents. Our modern interest in personality and the thought we have given to it have made us more aware than were the men of the fifth century of the deep and intimate union which two personalities may achieve. Is this as inadequate an analogy as the orthodoxy of the Council of Ephesus in 431 said it was? We are not quite sure that Nestorius has been adequately represented by his spokesmen and advocates, but it has appeared to many contemporary theologians that he was on the right track, and that his views were substantially vindicated by later developments. In any case, he failed to carry the day in 431, and was anathematized as heretical.

The Teaching of Eutyches

As often happens among zealous trackers-down of heresy, Nestorius's opposition soon overreached itself, and once more the balance swung in favor of a recognition of the full humanity of Jesus Christ. Eutyches, a monk of Constantinople and an ardent (perhaps so ardent as to miss his subtlety) disciple of Nestorius's formidable opponent, Cyril, found a new way to depreciate the Lord's humanity which seemed to avoid the formal charge of Apollinarianism. It was true, according to Eutyches, that a fully human nature entered into the Incarnate union, but after the union the human was utterly absorbed and lost in the divine.

The illustration that has been used is of pouring a cup of wine into the Mediterranean Sea. Although the wine was fully and really wine it simply lost all recognizable and identifiable character as wine when it became united with the waters of the Mediterranean Sea. The divine in Christ swallows up and obliterates in a similar way the human nature of Christ. The close union between human and divine, insisted upon in opposition to Nestorius, is now pressed to a point where the human after the union of the two is lost altogether.

Such a resolution of the problem was rejected and the grounds, one suspects, were really two. In the first place—and this is explicitly stated in the attacks on Eutyches—this idea of an obliterated humanity flies in the face of the Gospel picture of our Lord. As Pope Leo I pointed out in a famous tome, written expressly for the Council of Chalcedon, 451,

Each nature performs its proper functions in communion with the other; the Word performs what pertains to the Word, the flesh what pertains to the flesh. The one is resplendent with miracles, the other submits to insults . . . And so it does not belong to the same nature to say 'I and the Father are one' and 'the Father is greater than I.' [14]

Leo feels—as the opponents of Nestorius did not really feel—the impossibility of picturing the Lord of the Gospels—the Christ who prays to the Father in agony, "Let this cup pass from me"; the Christ who protests, "Why callest thou me good? There is none good save one, that is God"; the Christ who weeps at the tomb of Lazarus—as One whose divinity has swallowed up human finitude and the characteristic marks of human personality. Here, Leo's tome seems to say, is Apollinarianism in a new edition.

More serious, however, is the difficulty that such an understanding of the Incarnation implies the loss of human identity for the Christian who comes to share Christ's experience of God's grace and power in his life. "I am crucified with Christ; nevertheless I live," writes St. Paul. That is a text Eutyches never began to understand. "Nevertheless *I* live" means, as Reinhold Niebuhr has said,

[14] H. Bettenson, *op. cit.,* p. 72.

that, unlike other faiths which demand self-offering and self-sacrifice, Christianity does not result in an obliteration of the self but in a fulfillment and realization of the self. The Communist Party would urge its adherents to say "I am crucified with the revolution of the proletariat," but it would never insist on the adherent's adding, "Nevertheless, I live." The ideal of political totalitarianism is a yielding up of the self's independence and integrity on the altar of social revolution and social progress. Christianity does not picture human fulfillment in this way at all. "Nevertheless, I live," means that at the point of fullest union with God a man wills and thinks and acts still as an individual, albeit an individual whose whole delight is to do the divine will and fulfill the divine purpose.

The Monothelite Debate

This conviction, orthodox because it is rooted in the Christian experience of salvation and necessitated by it, gained fullest expression in the decision of the Church in the seventh century in what came to be called the "Monothelite" heresy. The hesitation to accept Christ's full humanity found here another expression by insisting that although one might agree with Leo that there continued to be a distinction in the Incarnate Christ between human and divine natures, there could be no distinction between the human and the divine wills. The human will must be judged to be wholly destroyed in the Incarnate Christ, where only the divine will had reality. The rejection of this conclusion was a kind of delayed victory for what appears to have been the main point of Nestorius, that a full and genuine human person must be acknowledged in the Incarnate Christ. Of course, this person was united to the Divine Person in a way and to a degree that can only be hinted at by even our highest moments of self-surrender and divine leading and inspiration, but the orthodox understanding of the Incarnation can best be grasped by beginning with our Christian experience of God in our own lives.[15] If it is true, as orthodox Church Fathers have not hesitated to say, that God became man in order that man might become divine, then there must be a close analogy between the Incarnation of Christ and every Christian man's experience of God's guidance and power and love.

Contemporary Christological Misconceptions

It was the rejection of this analogy and sharp distinction between the Incarnate Christ and Christian believers which lay behind the opposition to Nestorius; it has continued to haunt the Church ever since. From time to time the rediscovery of the Lord's full and real humanity has taken place, usually as a result of a fresh appreciation of the Gospel stories and of their picture of the Man Christ Jesus. The modern flowering of New Testament studies will, of course, profoundly affect the conception of Christ in the contemporary Church. But modern popular Christianity has not caught up with this scholarship, and the piety of too many Church people is still centered in a wholly unearthly and unreal divine figure who nowhere touches the common life of ordinary people. Miss Dorothy Sayers tells of her experiences in broadcasting, over the British Broadcasting Corporation, a series of radio plays about the life of Christ. She reports that the attempt of the series to render the Gospel account in terms of contemporary life met with widespread criticism and resentment, usually from devout church-goers. One irate listener objected to a Roman soldier saying to Christ in the scene in the guard room of Pilate's palace, "Aw, shut yer mouth." "Such an expression," said the listener, "was most jarring on the lips of one who was so close to our Lord." [16] Apparently to the minds of the pious, even the human enemies of

---

[15] This is the theme of one of the most illuminating modern discussions of the Incarnation, *God Was In Christ* by Donald M. Baillie (New York: Scribner's, 1948).
[16] See *The Man Born to Be King* (New York: Harper & Bros., 1949), p. 22.

Christ are invested with a stained-glass unreality and semi-divine character which removes them miles away from ordinary human affairs.

A similar tendency appears in some Roman Catholic apologia for the dogma of the Assumption. The argument runs something like this: the Virgin Mary's assumption into heaven is the necessary evidence of the true capacity and destiny of human nature. Christ's own resurrection and ascension are not sufficient to establish this since he was "a special case" and not "ordinary humanity," as was the case with St. Mary. This line of argument is wholly inconsistent with the message of the New Testament and with the great experience of salvation in Christ to which it bears testimony. The assurance of the epistle to the Ephesians is that God "hath quickened us together with Christ . . . and hath raised us up together and made us sit together in heavenly places in Christ Jesus." The phrase "the Body of Christ," used in the New Testament to mean the fellowship of his followers in the Church, is in itself proof of the close connection in the early Christian faith of the Incarnation and the regeneration and sanctification of the life of Christian men and women. Any theology which puts an insurmountable barrier between the Lord's humanity and ours, which treats him as such a special instance of the indwelling of humanity by the divine that ordinary men must look elsewhere for their hope of salvation, has made a mockery of the Christian experience and a nullity of the Christian Gospel. The two extremes of heresy—Arianism and any kind of Monophysitism (the doctrine that Christ's nature is simply or predominantly divine not human)—are the Scylla and Charybdis of Christian thought. To steer between the two, to stay within a central stream where both deity and humanity are fully and equally affirmed, is no less difficult today than in the fifth century. It is, however, no less necessary if Christ is to be known as our salvation.[17]

[17] See the note appended to this chapter on the doctrine of "Impersonal Humanity" in Christ, which seems to the author to be the sophisticated last stand of those who cannot really accept human personality in Christ.

The Doctrine of Atonement

This all becomes clear in the consideration of the way by which Christ saves men, a doctrine we usually call the Atonement. Here the question is not "Who is Christ?" but "What is it precisely that he did for us and how?" Obviously, however, the two questions are inseparably intertwined. When St. Anselm in the eleventh century wrote a treatise on the Atonement he gave it a title that reflected the orthodox doctrine of the Incarnation, *Cur Deus Homo* (Why God Became Man). Only a Christ such as orthodoxy had described could resolve a problem of man such as Anselm envisioned. The Church was right in giving priority to the question of who Christ was, for only when this is clearly understood can we begin to understand what he did.

The New Testament, the ancient Christian creeds, and the unanimous testimony of Christian faith and experience, all agree that the key and climax of Christ's saving work was the Cross and Resurrection. The complaint is sometimes heard that the creeds skip over the human life of Jesus Christ, moving immediately from the assertion of his birth to the description of his death. In a way, however, the same charge could be brought against the earliest of the Gospel accounts, St. Mark's Gospel. As soon as the evangelist has made it clear, through the stories of the recognition of Christ by the demons and the climactic confession of his messiahship by St. Peter, just who this person really is, the story at once points the reader toward Jerusalem. Unlike modern biographies, there is no leisurely examination of the growth and development of character, no delineation of important influences or formative ideas which moulded and shaped his thinking. The Gospel of St. Mark is content in the main with two things—who he is and what he did by his death and resurrection.

Just how this salvation of men was accomplished by his dying on the cross and his rising from the tomb the Gospels do not say and the rest of the New Testament gives only hints. St. Paul, who declares that his whole preaching centered in "Christ and him crucified," found in the Cross the supreme evidence of God's power both over the evil spirits abroad in the world and over the anxiety and pride which make human hearts so susceptible to their insidious and tempting influence. We have already seen how St. Paul pictured the whole creation as groaning under the burden of evil. The death and resurrection of Christ put these evil powers to flight and redeemed the original creation for its pristine purpose of serving and glorifying God and ministering to the needs of men.

The Pauline Doctrine

In much more detail, made even more interesting for us by its autobiographical flavor, St. Paul describes how the Cross of Christ delivers the center of man's personality from the besetting anxiety and self-centredness which we saw in the last chapter constitutes man's essential problem and defines his primary sin. St. Paul saw the Cross as the way by which God made known his unquestioning and all-embracing love for men. Here was the answer to man's desperate efforts to achieve self-importance and to clear his conscience. The answer of the Cross is that God has already assigned man an inestimable importance as his trusting and obedient son and that he has already accepted in advance all the failures of man to fulfill that relationship and has conferred on him this dignity which he never could merit or deserve. No way of self-salvation, no way from man to God, could escape the taint of self-concern and proud presumption which God's law of absolute love specifically rules out. For St. Paul only God can take the initiative in bringing man to himself, and by doing so in the Cross he has replaced man's anxiety with trust, his pride with love, his self-centredness with gratitude for the unbelievable gift. T. S. Eliot says in his play *The Cocktail Party,* "Your problem is not how to clear your conscience but how to learn to bear the burdens on your conscience." That is precisely the power which St. Paul believes the Cross of Christ conferred. To know Christ crucified for my sins brings an assurance, a boldness before God, and at the same time a trembling gratitude and an overflowing devotion which is just exactly that love of God which law and commandments could require but could never produce.

The early Church did not make much of this Pauline formulation of the Atonement. It found his less introspective treatment of the objective power of Christ over the evil spirits a more congenial way to express the meaning of the Cross and Resurrection. We are puzzled, we moderns, by the way in which the early Church speaks so easily and familiarly of evil spirits. We have already seen how the same idea has come alive for some contemporary Christians in such destructive mass movements as Naziism. For the early Christians both nature and history were filled with such spirits. Perhaps we can catch some of their meaning if we think today of the spirit of materialism or the spirit of conformity which have such power in our society. The early Church believed that Christ had broken the power of such spirits, that he had shown up their weakness and their pretension, that he had rescued men from fear of them and of their power. The drama of this victory was conceived of in vivid imagery in which the devil had been outmaneuvered by the Cross. Thinking Christ to be subject to his power of death, the devil had seized him as a fish seizes a baited hook, only to realize that he had fatally overreached himself and voided all his claims to the penalties of death against all other men forever. In the medieval drama the stirring climax was a scene called "the harrowing of hell," in which Christ burst asunder the gates of hades and triumphantly led forth the redeemed over the broken power of a defenseless devil. We have echoes of this "ransom to the devil" theory of the Atonement in our Easter hymns:

> He closed the yawning gates of hell;
> The bars from heaven's high portals fell;
> Let hymns of praise his triumphs tell!
> Alleluia!

The Weakness in Contemporary Thinking
about Atonement

It is a sign of weakness in contemporary thinking about the Atonement that this note of victory over evil has been largely missing. The major reason is the divorce between Good Friday and Easter in our preaching and thinking. Good Friday is depicted too often as that sad event in which the Son of God had to suffer and die in order to appease God's wrath and anger over our sins. (We shall see in a moment the truth in this understanding of the Cross). But, like many romantic novels, the story has a happy ending after all, and Easter tells us that our hero came through all right, and so we can forget about all the unpleasantness of Calvary. This is a dangerously heretical way to think of Easter and Good Friday. One does not follow another as the happy ending follows the perils and tribulations of the hero and heroine in romantic fiction. Easter and Good Friday are two sides of one and the same divine-human event.[18] Good Friday represents the perfect self-offering of a human life in absolute trust and love and obedience. Easter shows us that it is precisely such an offering which is the divinely empowered victory over the power of fear and self-centredness and faithlessness in the human heart. Easter is God's way of looking at Good Friday, and so St. John's Gospel always speaks of the Cross as the means of Christ's glorification and the Synoptic Gospels link

[18] The liturgical traditions of the Easter festival whereby the great act of joyful worship is the remembrance of his death and sacrifice, and amidst the lilies and the alleluias the faithful remember "the night in which he was betrayed" and receive sacramentally his glorified body and blood save traditional Christians from much modern sentimentality about Easter, which often becomes an unrelieved annual ecclesiastical "hurrah." On the other side, Good Friday ought not to be unrelieved gloom, and the custom in some places of tolling a bell thirty-three times at the end of the three-hour service seems a questionable way of marking the completion of his victorious sacrifice. T. S. Eliot speaks of the paradox of Christian worship where we "mourn and rejoice at the same time and for the same reason." This paradox ought to govern our worship if it is to reflect the paradox in which orthodoxy maintains its proportion and balance.

the Transfiguration with the prediction of the coming death of the Messiah. The Cross and the Resurrection show up the inadequacy of so much by which we live and the weakness of so much of what we fear. It assures men that their activities and undertakings can be purged of anxiety and pride and self-importance, and by God's mercy can be made a blessing and not a curse. So the evil in nature —disease and the cruel necessities of the natural order—and the evil in society—the spirit of conformity and greed, of tyranny over others and of limitless self-seeking—can be exorcized in the confidence of his victory over death and sin, of his showing up in the Cross and the Resurrection the weakness of the worst that wickedness and death can do to human faith and human love. This is the kind of assurance which the early Church gained from the Cross and the Resurrection and from their understanding of these events as a mighty victory over cosmic powers of evil which held men in thrall.

The "Moral Influence" *vs.* "Satisfaction" Theories

The other two classic theories of the Atonement did not overthrow the earlier theory; they rather probed its meaning more deeply and worked out its implications more fully. One of these theories directs our attention to the new power the Cross releases in men's hearts and minds; the other directs our attention to the new relationship which the Cross reveals and makes possible between God and man. Together they are both necessary in order to understand fully and appreciate deeply the meaning of Christ's work for us. The Church has never been very dogmatic about the Atonement, being content to say simply with the New Testament that "we were reconciled to God by the death of his Son." (Romans 5:10) The theory of how this was accomplished, while never having been dignified by formal recognition as a dogma, deserves our attention as an expression of the overwhelming majority of Christian people in all times and places.

The erratic mediaeval theologian Abelard is usually associated with what is the more popular of the two theories, often called "the moral influence" theory of the Atonement. It is not a very good name, for the theory does not deal exclusively with the moral influence which the contemplation of the Cross may create in human hearts. It deals rather with the whole transformation of outlook and attitude which such a contemplation accomplishes. Abelard said in effect that the Cross saves us by breaking down our pride and teaching us what havoc and suffering our sin creates in the world. The Cross is a measure of what we really do to one another and to God all the time. When we see the cost of our negligence and callousness, of our preoccupation with self and our indifference to others, how can we help but repent and ask for God's mercy which the Cross so generously bestows? Most of our modern hymns and modern Good Friday preaching reflect this meaning of the Atonement:

> When I survey the wondrous cross
> Where the young Prince of glory died,
> My richest gain I count but loss
> And pour contempt on all my pride.

> Were the whole realm of nature mine
> That were an off'ring far too small.
> Love so amazing, so divine,
> Demands my soul, my life, my all.

There is a moving version of Abelard's moral influence theory of the Atonement.

The chief heretical tendency in modern thinking about the Cross is to think that moral influence is enough, that all the Cross means or does is to produce contrition in the hearts of sinners. Even earlier than Abelard, however, another theologian saw that the Cross had to do more than that. St. Anselm's doctrine of the Atonement, sometimes called the "satisfaction theory," has seemed harsh and forbidding to some modern thinkers. Admittedly Anselm's language is not always persuasive in modern ears. He talks of God and man in the feudal language of master and serf. Sin is equated with failure to pay God the honor and service due him, and Anselm's main problem is how to make satisfaction to a God whose honor has been impugned. The usual modern reaction to his scruples is to say that real love never stands on its dignity but risks dishonor for the sake of reconciliation. Does not the doctrine of forgiveness solve all Anselm's problems?

This seems especially so because Anselm's solution sounds contrived and artificial. Sin, says Anselm, is a dishonor of infinite magnitude and one which man by himself can never make up. The enormity of dishonor is measured by the dignity and status of him to whom the dishonor is offered. To insult a king is a more heinous offense than to insult the local squire. What an incalculable insult sin must be, since it is the God of heaven and earth who is thereby offended. What is more, man can never even begin to make reparation for sin, for reparation means doing or giving something over and above what is due. But man owes God his love and service every moment of his existence. How can he ever establish any extra credit when he is already under such a total obligation? What man could never do for himself God who became man does for him. Because Christ is fully God his sacrificial death is infinitely meritorious, magnificent enough to overweigh the enormity of sin. Because Christ is fully man and can offer a perfect human life and suffer death as a penalty for sin although he knew no sin, his sacrifice avails on man's behalf and in his place. "He made there by his one oblation of himself once offered, a full, perfect and sufficient sacrifice, oblation, and satisfaction for the sins of the whole world."

What Must the Modern Christian Think?

Can modern Christians accept this Anselmic doctrine of the meaning of Christ's death? How can we answer those who say it presupposes a feudal God and an unreal substitution of one victim for another? A reply must begin by asking whether we have thought through all the meanings and implications of forgiveness. W. H. Auden paraphrases a prevalent heresy about forgiveness when he imagines a Christian saying, "God likes to forgive and I like to sin, so everything is admirably arranged." If this were all there were to the Christian idea of forgiveness, the Hindu objection to it as deeply immoral and demoralizing would appear to be amply justified. Recently a well-known college instructor was discovered to have participated in a large scale fraud on a television quiz program and to have perjured himself in testimony before a grand jury. He confessed his wrongdoing and told a congressional investigating committee that he was sorry. To the dismay of some of his students the Trustees of the University where he taught accepted his resignation. "Why?" asked the students. "He said he was sorry. Isn't that enough? Ought not the University practice the Christian virtue of forgiveness?" The answer is that mere contrition is *not* enough. The instructor had dealt a terrible blow to the standards of honesty and integrity on which a University is founded and built. For the University to wave aside this affront—not only to its honor but to its moral structure and purpose—would be to condone it and to suggest to the world that the University did not greatly care whether these standards were upheld or not. There was one way the young instructor might have been kept on the faculty. Some older and greater scholar, a light of the University and one of its chief claims to fame, might have stepped forward and offered to give up his job in the young instructor's place. For the University to accept such a sacrifice would make it clear beyond any doubt that it placed a terribly high price on moral integrity and it could therefore restore the young instructor to his post without appearing to condone his offense.

Anselm's picture of a God who is jealous of his honor and who can only forgive by some means which preserves the moral reputation of his universe is not, therefore, such a strange picture after all. No one who hears words of forgiveness from the Cross can say easily, "God likes to forgive." If the Cross is what forgiveness costs then the real frightfulness of man's offense is seen in its fullness. Only the Cross can speak of a God who hates sin but loves sinners. Only forgiveness by the Cross can save man from either complacency on the one hand or despair on the other.

These two doctrines of the Atonement belong together. Moral influence alone leads to sentimentality; satisfaction alone leads to mere legalism and artificiality. The God who pays the terrible price of forgiveness is the only God who can work the change in men's hearts that makes them loathe their sin for what it is and love and trust God with their whole being. Christ was sacrificed for us in order that we might be moved to join our sacrifice with his. One of the great collects of the Book of Common Prayer is the collect for the Second Sunday after Easter, and it expresses in a few lines the depth and range of what Christ means for the Christian:

Almighty God, who hast given thine only Son to be unto us both a sacrifice for sin, and also an ensample of godly life; Give us grace that we may always most thankfully receive that his inestimable benefit, and also daily endeavour ourselves to follow the blessed steps of his most holy life; through the same thy Son Jesus Christ our Lord. *Amen.*

To understand who Jesus Christ was and what he did for men is to grasp the great doctrines of the Christian faith. This understanding is not, of course, primarily intellectual; it is perfected in obedience and devotion and service. If that obedience is to be complete, however, if the devotion is to flame as it ought and the service is to be consistent and wholehearted, the Christian must believe that as the Son of God he came among us in the flesh, that he represents a full and complete union of God and man, proving the love of God and the potential dignity of man, that he died for our sins on the Cross and was highly exalted and given a name above every name. To such a Christ every knee must bow and every tongue confess that he is Lord to the glory of God the Father.

Appended Note on the Thesis of Impersonal Humanity

WIDELY accepted as orthodox has been the suggestion that while the full human nature of Christ must be affirmed, this does not mean—indeed cannot mean—that a human person or individual was involved in the Incarnation. Leontius of Byzantium suggested that in the case of Christ the principle of individuality was supplied by the Divine Person, the eternal Son, and that what was assumed by this Divine Person was an impersonal human nature and not a single personality. Indeed, it has been argued, if only one individual was involved in the Incarnation then only that individual could be saved whereas if one says that Christ assumed human *nature*, then all men may be saved. The reader may judge for himself what meaning can be attached to an impersonal human nature. Does this not leave unanswered the question of whether the heart and personal center of a man's existence can be redeemed? Is this not a kind of last stand of the opponents of a real humanity in the person of Jesus Christ? If one says, furthermore, that there was a full human will involved in the Incarnation (as the Church said against the Monothelites), is this not tantamount to saying that an individual was involved? What possible meaning could an "impersonal human will" have? Despite the popularity of this view, therefore, it seems to depend on a dubious supposition that there is a kind of generalized human nature in which all men share as if in a universal substance. This is a very special kind of philosophical idea and with our contemporary studies in individual psychology difficult to make much sense of. It does not appear to be a very useful approach in contemporary thought about the person of Christ.

CHAPTER SEVEN

The Life That
We Now Live

SOREN KIERKEGAARD once defined Christianity as consisting of three realizations: the abject humiliation of man, the infinite condescension of God, and the endless striving born of gratitude. Having considered how we ought to understand the meaning of the first two, we must now consider how to avoid serious misunderstanding of the nature of the third. What does it mean to live the Christian life? Of course, this is only preliminary to the task of self-discipline and resolution by which a truly Christian life is actually realized, but it is an important preliminary. One of the reasons why more people make no serious effort to live the Christian life is that they misunderstand so thoroughly what it really is. A wise priest once said that the clergy generally overestimated the understanding of their people and underestimated their resolution and good intentions. Instruction in what the Christian life really is—and incidentally what it is not—will be more wholesome and edifying than exhortations to try harder. Dr. Ferris, of Trinity Church, Boston, has said that many modern sermons sound like someone shouting swimming instructions to a man over-

139

board in mid-Atlantic! The man needs a life buoy more than he needs shouts of admonition and encouragement. St. Paul usually precedes his exhortations to his readers by a factual account of who they are, what God has done for them, and what the implications of all that are for their present problems of Christian living. In effect, St. Paul is saying, Be what you really are. Realize the meaning of what has happened to you. "If ye then *be* risen . . . seek those things that are above." Our purpose here is not to exhort or even to write in a manner intended to inspire or convert. Our purpose is to consider the implications for each of us in his ordinary life of the last two chapters on man's ruination and God's condescension.

Marks of the Christian Life

Contrary to the prevalent "peace of mind" cults which quite misrepresent the nature of the Christian life, the chief mark of the new life in Christ is warfare and struggle. "The flesh lusteth against the spirit, and the spirit against the flesh . . . so that ye cannot do the things that ye would." As St. Paul sees it Christians have more tensions than other people; they feel more deeply the conflict between God's purpose and the rebellion and self-assertion of human freedom. The war has become more serious to Christians, because it has found its major battle line right in the center of their own lives. "The life that we now live" is, according to St. Paul, a life in the flesh and yet a life lived by faith. "Flesh" for St. Paul is not just earthly existence, but earthly existence as man customarily and naturally lives it—proudly, aggressively, self-righteously, self-indulgently, self-centredly. A careful study of St. Paul will show that he nowhere promises a cessation of the warfare or a relaxation of the tension this side of our final resurrection. So the Christian life is a continuous and perennial death to sin and a rebirth to new possibility of life through God's forgiveness received again and again by faith and trust. That is why the Church never seems to weary of harping on the theme of sin and does not consider it overdoing things to provide a General Confession of sins every morning and every evening in the Prayer Book offices of Daily Morning and Evening Prayer. It is "new mercies each returning day" on which the Christian lives and in which he trusts. To grow in grace does not mean that we progressively root sin out of our lives. It means—as the testimony of the great saints makes abundantly clear—that we are progressively more aware of sin's subtleties, progressively more conscious of God's love and God's forgiveness, progressively bolder and less apprehensive as we live more fully by his power and grace. It has been said that the devil, when man proudly informs him that he is progressing, retorts, "Ah, yes, and I am progressing too." For every stage of spiritual growth there are appropriate sins, and as the history of even the most somber theologies shows, men can be proud of their humility and overbearing in their confidence of their forgiveness. Man never comes to the point where he can go it on his own in the Christian life. He needs God every hour, and to grow in grace is to learn to know how true that is.

The characteristic marks of the Christian life are not, therefore, the usual moral virtues. It would be quite difficult to show that Christians were more hard-working, more honest, more conscientious, more courteous, or even more chaste than non-Christians.[1] The Lambeth Pastoral Letter of 1958 was disarmingly frank on this point and said quite openly that "Christians are not better than other people but they serve a better Master." What does emerge distinctively within the Christian Church, however, is a new *quality* of moral life. The characteristic word the New Testament uses is "love," but it is to be defined by a cluster of other words that are often associated with it: forbearance, pity, forgiveness, kindness, compassion, and others of similar meaning. These are the qualities one would expect to develop within a community where

[1] The famous Kinsey Report did, of course, show that the violation of the sexual mores in such ways as indulging in premarital intercourse was significantly less frequent among practicing Jews and Christians than it was among the rest of the population. The inclusion of Jews shows, however, that this is not a Christian monopoly, and in any case the figures on sexual lapses are still high enough in the case of Christian Church members that no sweeping claims of moral superiority are justifiable.

man's unworthiness and God's mercy were the constant themes.
The late Dean Hughell Fosbroke called the Church "the Society
of the Forgiven." In their unique experience of sin and grace
Christians develop a peculiar attitude of self-understanding and of
acceptance and sympathy for others which gives their morality its
special characteristics.

The Doctrine of the Holy Ghost

This Christian life is measured and defined not only
by this new attitude toward one's neighbor but, of course, even
more fundamentally by a new attitude toward God. The realization
that he has done everything for us, that even at the highest moments of spiritual achievement "every virtue we possess, and every
victory won, and every thought of holiness are his alone," is expressed by Christians in the doctrine of the Holy Ghost. The chief
modern heresy, it is sometimes said, concerning the Holy Ghost
is to neglect him altogether. More sermons, we are told, ought to be
preached about the Holy Ghost, more hymns addressed to him,
more attention paid to his works. The fact that the festival of
Pentecost is never able to match in ecclesiastical glamor or popular
excitement the festivals of Christmas and Easter is taken as a bad
sign, evidence that our devotion and piety are one-sided and inadequate. Perhaps so. We have already seen in our discussion about
the Trinity that, apart from the doctrine of the Holy Ghost, Christians tend to think of God either as "way up there" (the Father)
or "way back then" (Jesus). The doctrine of the Trinity, however,
does not imply that each of the Persons must receive equal attention. The New Testament does not seem to be at any pains to parcel
out attention with strict equality. Indeed, if we understand the
Trinity in the orthodox sense, we must see the point of St. Augustine's observation that in his operations toward that which is outside himself the Trinity cannot be divided up or separated. One of

the reasons modern Christians are so vague about the Holy Ghost[2]
is that they try to picture him apart from God the Father and God
the Son. In the New Testament he is "the Spirit of our Lord Jesus
Christ," and New Testament Christians would be unable to tell you
about any particular moment of their spiritual lives whether it was
the Holy Ghost or Christ himself, who was their inspiration and
the abiding presence in whose companionship they lived. The point
is it would be quite heretical to try to make any such distinction.
God the Holy Ghost is with us in every moment in which our Lord
is remembered, felt to be present and powerful. He is with us in
every intimation of the reality and mighty working of God in nature
and history. The Persons of the Trinity are not jealous of each
other, all pushing forward for equal attention! "He that hath seen
me hath seen the Father," our Lord said, and the Holy Ghost would
say the same. "I will not leave you comfortless," said the Johannine
Christ, "I will come to you." He spoke in this context of the Holy
Ghost. Christians believe in one God, indivisible in his operations,
and they need not worry overmuch whether each of the personal
roles in which this Triune God exists and works receives equal
mention.

The Nature of the Church

The unanimous testimony of the early Christians was
that this God met them most surely and most fully and most
powerfully within the life of the Christian community which is the
Church. The life that we now live we live in the Church. We believe
in God the Holy Ghost, who draws us into a community and who

[2] Surely "Holy Ghost"—for all its connotations of Hallowe'en spooks—is
a better term than "Holy Spirit," for spirit is a word that is almost hopelessly synonymous with vagueness. The writer remembers gratefully a
kindly professor who told him that in his translation of German on an
examination he had "caught the spirit of it." Obviously here the word "spirit"
was the opposite of precise or exact! At least the word "ghost" has personal implications.

reveals himself to us in that community and bestows power and insight for the task of living the life of that community. One of the results of the biblical doctrine of man has been a highly developed sense of individualism in our culture, but this individualism—expressed, for example, in the fact that one becomes a Christian by a highly personal act in which he is given a name as an individual —can grow to an heretical extreme in which one conceives of Christianity as primarily what I decide to do about Christ and his teachings. A distinguished colleague of Franklin Delano Roosevelt's, writing of his religion, said that the late president "believed firmly in Christian principles and tried to put them into practice whenever possible." It would be difficult to contrive a definition of Christianity which would be more unintelligible to the first-century Christians. They began with the life of the Christian community, not with individual belief and self-conscious effort. As J. B. Phillips has said, they regarded Christianity more as an experience than as a performance, as something which had laid hold of them and possessed them rather than as a program they had laid out for themselves and were trying to follow whenever possible. "They were full of the Holy Ghost." Almost every significant decision and action in the Acts of the Apostles is preceded by that explanation.

Modern attempts to justify dispensing with the Church as a necessary part of the Christian life are not usually to be taken very seriously. They are more often excuses for laziness or preoccupation and very seldom show any disciplined determination to manifest private Christianity. Those who profess to be able to worship God in the garden or on the golf course do not usually do so but—probably wisely—concentrate on gardening or playing golf, which is after all what they are there for. A garden or a golf course does afford, as a matter of fact, some opportunities for meditation on the glories of creation and perhaps in the case of the latter on the frailties of man, but Christianity is much more specific in its object of devotion. It centers in the story of God's act on our behalf in Jesus Christ, and one does not hear that story recounted except in church. Having once heard it recounted, one may recall it in the midst of any kind of circumstances, but men need specific moments when it is regularly and uninterruptedly recalled and its meaning and implications allowed to penetrate and when all of human life is consciously offered as a way of fulfilling its significance. This is what Christian worship does and what undisciplined meandering thoughts about God in garden or golf course never succeed in doing.

There is a deeper reason for the Church, of course, and it is closely related to the very objections and criticisms that are often made of it. The fact that we do not find the people we meet in church entirely congenial may be just the reason why the Church rather than our usual social groups is the most appropriate setting for the exercise of Christian love. Of course, we hasten to say, Christian love must judge and ultimately determine the character of all our relationships. Most of our relationships, however, begin with some human bond of sympathy or natural congeniality. Family ties, business association, similarity of background, taste and temperament—these are the foundations of the ordinary groups in everyday life. If Christian love, however, is really to be put to its test and to have its most characteristic expression, there must be some social group where none of these natural bases of human association is necessarily present and where nevertheless there is mutual respect and understanding and concern. It is the peculiar glory of the Christian Church to be a society of rather uncongenial and curious people who have only one thing in common, and that is the great love they have for God, who has given them so much in Jesus Christ. God's love for us reached across the terrible gulf of uncongeniality which the crucifixion of Christ symbolizes, and so we must respond and reproduce that love in some society in which the most unlikely people in the world become our brothers. St. Paul can never get over the way in which the Church brings together men and women who would naturally find almost nothing in common—bond servants and free Roman citizens, rude barbarians and cultivated Greeks, Jews and Gentiles—and makes them fellow-members of a society so close-knit that it must be compared to a family household. Just because that could happen nowhere else but in the Church, the Church is indispensable as a part of the Christian experience.

The Heresy of Denominationalism

It is this truth about the Church that makes the modern heresy of denominationalism (or even worse, parochialism) such an insidious and dangerous one. What a travesty it is on Christianity really that a man in Christendom today is allowed the subversive luxury of picking out a church he "likes." How destructive it is of the fulness of Christian truth and of Christian fellowship and community to have groups of Christians withdrawing from one another on the basis of doctrinal specialization or ecclesiastical preference, so that, for example, all the Christians who understand the power and presence of God in silence form themselves together as Quakers over here and all those who know the rich values of ordered liturgical worship and sacramental grace draw together as Anglicans or Roman Catholics or something else over there. If the Church were true to her real nature and mission, it would make a fetish out of uncongeniality and deliberately seek to bring together the most unlikely people so that they might hear each other testify what Christ means to them. The movement for Christian reunion is not really an elective in the curriculum of Christian living; it is required by the very nature of the Church itself and by the undiscriminating and all-embracing love of God in Christ. Christians may differ as to the way in which reunion is to be achieved and means by which the reality of Christian unity is to be expressed, but no Christian can defend the present system of autonomous and unintegrated denominations except at the peril of dangerous heresy.[3] Only when it is seen to be deeply subversive of the Chris-

[3] Even less defensible, of course, is racial segregation, and it is not dealt with at length here because almost all major Christian bodies are on record (whatever their present practice may be) as to its incongruity in the Church of Christ. The argument sometimes heard that a man has a right to choose

tian experience of grace and reconciliation will the present situation
be attacked with the vigor and imagination it requires.

We have now come, however, into an area where the question
of heresy *vs.* orthodoxy is complicated by the contemporary ecclesiastical situation. The doctrines considered before this point
have had no particular denominational characteristics. A Baptist
can be an Apollinarian heretic about the person of Christ as
readily as an Anglican can. To talk about heresies concerning the
nature of the Church is, however, a somewhat different matter,
for here the great divisions of Christendom hold widely differing
views. On this single subject of the Church—and the closely related questions of the ministry and sacraments—Christendom is
more divided than on any other subject. To talk about heresy and
orthodoxy here is to stir up a hornet's nest of passionate debate, a
debate in which the sides are determined very largely by the particular ecclesiastical background of the individual concerned. Here
more than elsewhere we ought to remember an early warning in
this book against premature accusations of heresy. Orthodoxy
about the nature of the Church is only beginning to emerge into
view. It is not a question that has once for all been settled. Almost
all Christian groups except the Roman Catholics are involved in
anomalies and ambiguities in their ecclesiastical practice that be-
tray the lack of any clear line of doctrine about the Church. We
are thinking here on the front lines of the modern Christian attack
on a complicated and perplexing problem.

We have already seen that the Church lives in a paradoxical
way, never fully realizing what she is meant to be, living in the flesh
and yet possessed by the Spirit of God himself. This paradox is
apparent in the New Testament itself. What shall we make, asks the
First Epistle of St. John, of the Christians who have separated
themselves from us? The answer is perhaps too simple a one to be
very useful, but it is quite simply that they never were really
Christians in the first place. The Gospel of St. Matthew records a

---

the people with whom he worships is flatly in contradiction to the whole
tradition of orthodoxy about the nature of the Church and does not deserve
the dignity of refutation.

parable of our Lord's which seems, however, to reflect more naturally a problem of the later Church. What about the weeds that
spring up in the wheat field, which is to say, what shall we make of
the presence of unworthy members within the visible fellowship
of the body of the Church? And even a cursory reading of St. Paul's
epistles will reveal the paradox between the way he speaks of the
Church in principle—"elect of God, holy and beloved"—and the
way he rebukes them for the worst kinds of sins and shortcomings
—divisions, fornication, contentiousness, and suchlike. For St.
Paul to call the Church the Body of Christ does not mean that he
is under any illusions as to how its members behave themselves.
They are "holy and beloved," but they are also entangled in terrible sin and need frequent and sharp talk, at which St. Paul was
something of a specialist.

The Church, Visible and Invisible

Out of this paradox there developed the doctrine of
the distinction between the Visible and the Invisible Church. Part
of the responsibility for working out this distinction was St. Augustine's, who was the first Christian thinker after the New Testament period to reflect seriously and deeply about the nature of the
Church. He began by analyzing the problem of society in terms of
the inner purpose and motive which underly it, and he concluded
that there were two possibilities in principle: either a society was
organized for the purpose of serving and loving God to the denial
of, or indifference to, self or else it was organized for the purpose of
serving and loving the self to the denial of, or indifference to, God.
In principle the Church was the first kind of society, indeed the
only one of this kind, for only in the Christian Church were to be
found the power and grace which enabled a man truly to love God.
Augustine was too much of a realist not to appreciate the fact that
only in principle was the Church this kind of society. In fact, the
Church as we see it and know it has, as St. Augustine specifically
points out, many people in it who do not really share in this

spiritual principle of its life and, indeed, has outside its membership many professed enemies who are destined finally to come into its fellowship and to share fully in its spirit. So Augustine must distinguish between the Church as we see it and the Church as it exists full and complete in the mind of God, "without spot or wrinkle or any such thing." [4]

The Heresy of Papal Infallibility

As in many other areas of discussion, the problem in the understanding of the Visible and the Invisible Church is to hold the truth in both conceptions and not to wander into a heresy, on the one hand, which exalts the visible organization at the expense of realism and honest self-criticism, or into a heresy, on the other hand, which dismisses problems of church life and organization as essentially irrelevant for the building up of the Christian life. The first is the heresy of Roman Catholicism, especially evident since the decree of Papal Infallibility of 1870. The second is the heresy of much sectarian-minded Protestantism, especially evident in the splintering tendencies of spiritualistic individualism which has produced more than 250 so-called Protestant groups in the American society. The essence of the Papal Infallibility heresy is that although individual Roman Catholics may and do sin and make mistakes about the faith, the Church herself, at her official and spiritual center, acting through the divinely appointed Chief Pastor, cannot err in any essential matter. The language used about the Pope's status and power on such occasions of official teaching is unlimited. He stands in Christ's place and what he says has exactly the same sacrosanct character as the words of Christ himself. This doctrine has no bearing whatever on the Pope's personal life. He may be a notorious sinner and evil-liver—Roman Catholics may admit that several Popes have made rather a name for them-

---

[4] Part of St. Augustine's conviction here is based on his strong belief in Predestination, consideration of which is reserved to an appended note at the end of this chapter.

selves in this respect—but by a special miracle of grace, comparable to the Incarnation itself, even the worst of Popes is preserved from error when teaching officially on matters of faith and morals. This is heretical chiefly because it is so inconsistent with the nature of faith and with the whole history of God's dealings with man. We have here the same image as in biblical fundamentalism—a divine oracle to which the response is to be uncritical and unquestioning obedience. It would be impossible to render this in any kind of human analogy that would not make it absurd. What friendship, what marriage, what relation of father and son—and all these analogies are used in the Scriptures for the relationship of Christ to his Church—would be conceivable in the terms which the doctrine of Papal Infallibility sets up? The premium is placed on credulity rather than on response to the revelation of the heart of the other and subsequent commitment in trust and faith. The mystery which characterizes all personal relations—and therefore supremely characterizes God's dealings with men—is here dispelled, and revelation becomes a public pronouncement and faith unquestioning acceptance. Is it conceivable that the God, who in his supreme self-revelation in Jesus Christ, spoke only in parables, refused to parade his divine power, gave only hints of his divine nature and truth, and made his greatest appeal to men in the weakness and ambiguity of the Cross should now, some 1900 years later, cast aside all reticence and come thundering forth with infallible utterances placarded in black and white which leave man no alternatives but stunned obedience or resentful scepticism? Papal Infallibility is not only demonstrably untrue historically (for some Popes have made embarrassingly heretical judgments) but it is wholly out of keeping with the Christian idea of God, of man, of faith, and of true religion. No wonder that it caused such a profound shock in the Roman Catholic Church and caused heart-searching dismay among so many Roman Catholic leaders.[5]

---

[5] For a full and readable treatment of the origins of this doctrine see Geddes MacGregor's *The Vatican Revolution* (Boston: Beacon Press, 1957).

The Heresy of Individualism

Potentially less dangerous, because less formally and officially defined, is the heresy of the opposite sort which depreciates the importance of the life of the Visible Church and makes religion consist altogether in the genuine allegiance of the individual heart to God. There is truth here, of course, which must be pressed against any mechanical or sociological concepts of salvation. Men are not saved by sacraments or by membership in a visible society if those sacraments and that membership do not generate trusting faith and devotion. But in their desire to underline this truth, movements again and again in Church history have made the Church so indefinable that it has ceased to seem related at all to the process of salvation. The Church is a kind of afterthought for this sort of sectarianism. Those who have already been saved—and the role of the Church in this process is quite overlooked—draw themselves together to form the Church. As a condition of membership one must recount his salvation experience and usually this experience is of a highly personal kind which has no organic relationship to church life.

The fruits of this view of the Church are likely to be a steady depreciation of its worship, its sacraments, and its characteristic life and fellowship. These are hard words, I am sure, to many Protestants whose roots are in this sect-type Church tradition, but the contemporary loss of Protestant identity, the carelessness of habits of worship, the absence of a strong sacramental emphasis with a consequent loss of focus and structure for Christian devotion, all seem to many observers to be all too characteristic of much contemporary Protestantism of this sort. This loss of vitality is often obscured by the Church's assuming other functions as a counselling, or character-building, or socializing influence in the community, but the central purpose for which the Church exists—namely, to fashion the likeness of Christ in the hearts and lives of his people—

is done so casually and haphazardly as to fail of any real fulfillment. The Church is both visible and invisible, but only through the visible organism with its authorized ministry, its authentic Scriptures, its creeds and confessions, its sacraments, and its living tradition of worship does the invisible fellowship grow up. The Church Visible is the agent of God the Holy Spirit, by which men are brought into the Church Invisible. St. Augustine, who held so firmly to the idea of the Church as an invisible society, was also, it must be remembered, a diocesan bishop who was at pains to maintain and set forward Catholic tradition in worship and doctrine and sacramental life.

One of the most important doctrinal controversies in which St. Augustine was involved grew out of this unshakable conviction he had about the validity and significance of the Visible Church. It revolved around a heresy known as Donatism, which was a product of a strict and rather moralistic Christian movement in North Africa, which broke off relationships with other Christians on the grounds that their clergy were incapacitated by reason of moral and spiritual deficiencies. Specifically they refused to accept as bishop a man who under the threat of persecution had weakened so far as to hand over the Scriptures to the authorities to be destroyed. Such a lapse does seem a rather serious handicap to a man who is to exercise effectively the authority of the office of a bishop, but the reaction of the Donatists in declaring that the Church and its clergy were only to be accepted insofar as they measured up to certain preconceived moral standards was one which, in effect, undermined all church order and church authority. Although sympathetic in many ways with the Donatist criticisms of the rather low level of piety and devotion which had begun to characterize the Church after Constantine, St. Augustine saw that a Visible Church that was to exercise the kind of widespread responsibility which was now being placed upon it by the successors of Constantine could not rest its claims to authority on such grounds as the Donatists proposed.

The Authority of the Church

What is the basis of the authority of the Church? Many modern Christians would answer "success." It is notable how much respect can be gained by religious groups of the most dubious antecedents and the most questionable theological quality simply because, as is said, "it is successful in reaching people." More thoughtful and serious Christians, who are nevertheless of the Donatist persuasion though they may never have heard the name, would answer in terms of spiritual earnestness and moral intensity. But even this will not do, for it places the Church's authority on grounds so subjective as to invite continual schism and to produce a generation of drifting Christians who join a church because the minister is likeable, the location convenient, or the Sunday School or Women's Society has the most popular program or congenial membership. Of course, one prays and works for a Church of deep spirituality and moral power, and one which commends in every possible way its Gospel to men. It has been said that the Gospel itself is offensive enough to modern thinking not to add the offensiveness of personal ineptitude and ineffectiveness. But such personal considerations are not a proper basis for judging the Church's *authority*. All that we have said about the Church on its human side, being a very frail and often rather unimpressive institution, leads to the conviction that its authority rests on the Gospel it preaches and the sacraments it administers, on the ideal it holds up, the Christ it exalts, and on nothing else. The Visible Church—not to be confused, of course, with the Invisible Church—is not identified by what it practices but by what it preaches. It may be stimulating to urge men to practice what they preach; it would be disastrous to urge as a corollary that one preach only as much as he can put immediately into practice. The Church is often condemned because it has preached so effectively the superlative ideal which is Christ and so is measured by its own message. That is as it should be. It creates the sort of tension and self-criticism which is healthy, but it must never be forgotten that the primary responsibility of the Church is the preaching which creates that tension and begets that perennial criticism. The Thirty-nine Articles define the Church as the place where the Gospel is truly preached and the sacraments duly administered, and specifically condemns the heresy that "the unworthiness of a minister" hinders the efficacy of a sacrament. In our age of anarchic individualism, Donatism runs rampant and needs continual rebuke, but a rebuke which does not, on the other hand, produce ecclesiastical pride and complacency.

It is significant that the historic Creeds ask the Christian to *believe* in the Church. That is in some ways a curious request. It might be expected that one would be asked to belong to the Church, but what can it mean to believe in it? It is the Creeds' way of saying that the Church in many important ways is invisible but that one must believe that the invisible fellowship is truly and verily being built up in the visible life of the Church as we see and know it. The late Archbishop Temple is reported to have said that he believed fervently in the Holy Catholic Church and only regretted that it did not at present exist. He was saying in a striking way that the Church in its perfection is invisible, that as a matter of sober historic fact she is at the present time divided and rent asunder. Catholicity, unity, holiness, and apostolicity are marks of a Church which does not at the moment exist as a concrete historical institution. It is something we trust in and believe in and work for and pray for. What is more we are convinced that in the life of the Church Visible, for all its faults and blemishes—and the great collect of Archbishop Laud [6] frankly admits that the Church can be and often is in error, divided, and in other ways far less than what it should be—God is calling, pardoning,

[6] "O Gracious Father, we humbly beseech thee for the holy Catholic Church; that thou wouldest be pleased to fill it with all truth, in all peace. Where it is corrupt, purify it; where it is in error, direct it; where in any thing it is amiss, reform it. Where it is right, establish it; where it is in want, provide for it; where it is divided, reunite it; for the sake of him who died and rose again, and ever liveth to make intercession for us, Jesus Christ, thy Son, our Lord."

commissioning, saving men and women into that eternal fellowship whose exact constituency he alone can know. This is what it means not just to belong to the Church but to *believe* in it.

The Church's Ministry and Sacraments

One of the serious consequences of the sectarian heresy is that it minimizes the importance, and underestimates the difficulties, of achieving the visible unity of the Church. Since the Church is on this view largely an invisible community of souls, united already in Christ by a common faith in him and devotion to him, sectarian-minded Protestantism tends to dismiss the problem of organic reunion as either undesirable or to be attained with a few gestures of mutual respect and comradeship. Some American churches advertise themselves as "interdenominational" as if the historic differences of creeds, of ministry, of sacramental faith and practice could be waved aside and Catholic unity achieved overnight by an isolated congregation. What is worse such cavalier attempts are labelled "ecumenical" although the responsible ecumenical movement of our time has always faced frankly the formidable problems involved in any such achievement. To say that the problem of an authorized ministry, for example, is one which can simply be ignored in the effort to be "ecumenical" is to fly in the face of hundreds of years of Church history and amounts, in effect, to accepting the sectarian version of the Church. The traditional Catholic view of the ministry has been that through the office of a single bishop in each geographical area the continuity and unity of the Church is safeguarded and preserved. This bishop's continuity with the past is guaranteed by the necessity of his consecration by three other bishops and the unity of the Church in his area of responsibility is guaranteed by his authority as Chief Pastor and as the sole person qualified to ordain to the ministry. Some would claim that this arrangement, which is called the monarchical episcopate, is set forth in the New Testament itself. Others would make a more defensible claim, namely that

it emerged in the Church within a generation of the end of the
New Testament period and so comes to us with the weight of a
1900 year history and with advantages of a pastoral and spiritual
sort that are obvious.[7] Anglicanism in the providence of God,
which works through the ambiguities of history (and what could
be more ambiguous than the marital history of Henry VIII or the
political ambitions of Elizabeth I), has retained this Catholic arrangement of the ministry and believes that no proposals for
Christian reunion can succeed which do not include it in its es-
sentials. One can make this claim and hold this conviction without for a moment calling into question the spiritual reality of other
ministries, but one cannot hold it and be content with an easy-
going dismissal of the whole problem of an authorized ministry
as irrelevant and picayune. At the heart of many of the problems
which beset contemporary Protestantism is a kind of lurking Donatism which makes spiritual effectiveness the only mark of authority
and so leaves the Visible Church floundering in uncertainty over
its structure and responsibility. Anglicans may not be able to
commend the historic episcopate to the rest of Protestant Christendom, but they are duty-bound to insist that until the question
of recognized authority in the ministry is faced and resolved organic reunion is an impossibility.

Transubstantiation

Many of the questions about the Visible and Invisible Church reappear in the discussions about the characteristic
acts of the Church in its sacramental life. The two extremes of

---

[7] The Lambeth Conference of 1920 chose this more modest approach when
it asked in its Pastoral Letter "To All Christian People": "May we not
reasonably claim that the Episcopate is the one means of providing such
a ministry" [i.e., a ministry, as the Letter says, "acknowledged by every part
of the Church as possessing not only the inward call of the Spirit but also
the communion of Christ and the authority of the whole body"]? Cf. H. Bettenson, *op. cit.*, p. 444.

heretical opinion about the nature of the Church are found in the area of sacramental theology. A sacrament according to the Anglican Prayer Book is "an outward and visible sign of an inward and spiritual grace." That definition sets the problem of what sacraments really are and do in the same familiar terms in which we have been thinking about the Church herself. What is the relation between the visible and invisible, the outward and the inward? Not surprisingly, Roman Catholicism and sectarian Protestantism fall into opposite heresies. The Roman Catholic heresy is enshrined in the dogma of transubstantiation, which asserts that the physical entities of bread and wine do not simply convey the grace and power of the divine life but actually become, by metaphysical transformation, what they signify, represent, and transmit. Just as the human nature in the Incarnate Christ loses its identity and integrity in the union with the Divine, just as the human capacities and frailties of the papal mind are annulled by the infallible working of the Holy Spirit, so now in sacramental theology we are told that the bread and wine are in essence destroyed and obliterated and replaced by the very Body and Blood of the glorified Christ.

There are many grounds on which this dogma of transubstantiation may be attacked. One of them, at least, is philosophical in character. The dogma distinguishes between essence and accidents, between that which makes a thing what it is and that which is purely coincidental and nonessential. A table in the room where this is written has four legs, is made of natural-colored wood, and is about two and one-half feet high. All those things might be different, and the object in the room would still be a table. It might be metal and not wood, black and not natural-colored, wider, longer, or higher. But there would have to be some feature about it—we might call it "table-ness," the ability to hold something up from the floor—which makes it what it is and the absence of which would indeed leave us with no table at all but something different. This "tableness" is its essence, and the color, material, and size are its accidents. Transubstantiation affirms that only the accidents of bread and wine remain after the consecration. On philosophical grounds one might ask how the consecrated elements can then be identified as bread and wine, as they obviously appear to be. For if the thing that makes them what they are is so invisible and unobservable that it can be destroyed without anyone being the wiser, then how were we able to identify them as bread and wine in the first place? An essence must be something observable or else it fails of its purpose, which is to identify the object in question. Transubstantiation appears to be involved in impossible philosophical absurdities even on its own grounds.

The more serious argument against it is that it overthrows, as the Thirty-nine Articles say, the nature of a sacrament and, as they might have added, the whole doctrine of creation and of the nature of Christian faith. Transubstantiation is a refutation of the sacramental principle which declares that physical objects, acts, and relationships can convey spiritual truth, power, and reality. The early Church Father, Irenaeus, spoke of the Eucharist as "proclaiming harmoniously the unity of flesh and spirit." [8] Transubstantiation says in effect that the flesh cannot really participate in this unity until it is destroyed in its essence and replaced by something else. At the very heart of Christian worship, this dogma says, earthly things will not do and by a special miracle are obliterated and destroyed with only their accidents remaining. As a consequence the mood of worship is no longer that of perceiving in physical things the providence and love of God—the kind of insight and heightened perception which is inspiration and faith —but that of credulity before an impossible metaphysical proposition.

[8] Cf. the full quotation in H. Bettenson, *op. cit.,* p. 105, where Irenaeus says: ". . . the bread of the earth, receiving the invocation of God, is no longer common bread but Eucharist, consisting of two things, an earthly and a heavenly." Transubstantiation would correct Irenaeus by saying that the earthly has in reality been destroyed, and we are victims of a delusion if we think that both really exist together.

The Sacraments as Mere Signs

In reaction to this heresy, Protestant sacramental theory has, however, sometimes gone to the opposite extreme and spoken of sacraments as mere symbols. It is difficult to know exactly what a "mere" symbol is. Symbols are usually—if they are valued and used—not "mere" at all, but powerful and effective, and as "real" as anything else in the world of man's experience. It is a curious fact—due perhaps to our scientific ways of thinking and speaking—that we should say that a thing is "only a symbol." The sexual relation between husband and wife is, of course, a symbol of their devotion and care and love for one another. Unless it is this, it is merely an animal relationship. But would anyone depreciate the sex act between a devoted husband and wife on the ground that after all it is only a symbol? It is the most powerful and dynamic and profoundly moving thing that could be imagined. In one sense, a sacrament is a symbol. Unless it is, one must have recourse to some theory such as transubstantiation. But it is not a "mere" symbol but a powerful and effective symbol, a divinely appointed means by which God acts and moves within the lives of faithful men and women. The outward and visible sign becomes the vehicle and means whereby the inward and spiritual grace is as a matter of experience conveyed, sealed, and assured.

The heresy implicit in the theory of the sacraments held in some sectarian type Protestant groups is that the physical is in no real way the means or vehicle of the spiritual but only represents that which is already conveyed and transmitted in other ways. Just as the Visible Church for such thinkers is not really the way by which the Invisible Church is built up and established but only a mere symbol of it, so—not surprisingly—the sacraments are similarly treated. The sacraments for some Protestants are signs which represent that which is absent or which comes in some other way. The sacraments in the main Christian tradition are rather thought of as symbols which convey and transmit precisely that which they represent. So in the service of the Holy Communion, in the Book of Common Prayer, we pray that God may "bless and sanctify with thy Word and Holy Spirit, these thy creatures of bread and wine; that we, receiving them according to thy Son our Saviour Jesus Christ's holy institution, in remembrance of his death and passion, may be partakers of his most blessed Body and Blood." Such a prayer is wholly inconsistent both with transubstantiation and with any theory of empty symbolism. It makes it clear that God the Holy Spirit, working through precisely these physical things used in our devout remembrance of Christ's own life and death and resurrection, is the guarantor of the divine presence and power, and the means by which the reality of Christ's own life is born and nurtured in us.

The Life of Perfect Freedom

The life that we now live as Christians is both definable and precise as to structure and focus, and indefinable and mysterious as to range and profundity. It consists in sacramental worship and membership in a concrete visible social organism which is the Christian Church on earth. On the other hand, the wind of the Holy Spirit "bloweth where it listeth," and every man discovers his own way to be a Christian and expresses his faith in terms of his own talents and his own weaknesses. Nowhere is there more encouragement given to individuality and at the same time more emphasis on fellowship and corporate unity than in the Church—and perhaps most particularly in the Church at worship. In the life of the Eucharist, for example, man is more of an individual and yet more closely knit into the fabric of a society of his fellows than in any other experience of his existence. In the offertory he carries into the divine presence the work of his own hands which, in important ways, is nevertheless also the work of his society. The sins that are confessed are the sins of the groups and fellowships of which he is a part—his church, his city, his nation, his world—and yet they are also his own sins, which have intensified and complicated the corporate sins of mankind. The forgiveness and new power which come in the communion are for the sake of the Church, that it may more truly and more adequately preach the Gospel and minister the sacraments, and yet they are for him too that he may grow in the deepest center of his personal self more and more into the likeness of Christ.

In our lonely and atomized society the fashion of our thought may very well become excessively social so that we overdo the corporate aspect of the Christian life and minimize the ways in which individual Christians may indeed manifest very odd and eccentric gifts of the Holy Spirit. As C. S. Lewis has pointed out,[9] however, St. Paul's analogy of the Church as a human body does not presuppose that every member will be an exact duplicate of every other but rather the contrary. The point is that each member in his radical individuality, making just that contribution which he alone can make, is absolutely indispensable to the healthy functioning of the whole organism. This is dramatically experienced in the Church's liturgical worship which is the very heart and center of the Christian life. I am one with my fellows and with angels and archangels and with all the company of heaven, and yet I speak to God by myself and for myself and with a self-scrutiny matched in no other human experience. The Church voices contrition and aspiration which go far beyond my comprehension and shame my complacency and my coldness of heart, and yet I understand one surpassing fact which no one else can ever know —how graciously God has dealt with me. This is the great function of Christian worship: to enable me to be myself and to belong also to my fellows. It accomplishes the purpose of the Christian life—to depend more and more upon God and in that dependence to find perfect freedom.

[9] Cf. his essay on the Body of Christ in *The Weight of Glory*.

Appended Note on
Predestination

THE Anglican article on Predestination, sometimes cited as a prime example of the genius of Anglicanism for double-talk, makes nevertheless an important point by beginning with the place that the consideration of Predestination plays in the Christian life. It is "full of sweet and godly comfort." That is the way to begin to think about this thorny subject—from the point where I have known God's prevenience and sustaining grace in my own religious life. Anyone who is a Christian will know of many instances which prove that God sought him before he ever dreamt of seeking God. The Catechism speaks of the "state of grace unto which it hath pleased God to call me," and every Christian knows something of what that means. Parents, teachers, friends, clergy, the combination of circumstances—all these have seemed to conspire to lead us into the Christian life and to deeper and broaden our discipleship at unforgettable moments.

The difficulty comes when we begin to wonder why others do not quite manage to receive the same sort of guiding and leading and enlightening. To attempt to resolve this difficulty by saying that God made up his mind beforehand quite without any reference to the responses of the human beings in question that some would receive his guidance and grace and others never would seems plainly heretical.[10] It cannot be made consistent with God's love, no matter how ingenious the attempts have been.

The difficulty lies in part in the prefix "pre." That is misleading, for God's purposes are neither *before* or *after* our decisions and actions

[10] This would appear to be the position taken up by the Calvinists at the Synod of Dort in 1618 where a more moderate statement of the doctrine of Predestination by a Dutch theologian called Arminius was condemned. In many ways, the view set forth in this appended note follows the Arminian line more than the line of the Synod of Dort. Cf. samples of the Arminian views in H. Bettenson, *op. cit.*, pp. 375-377.

but rather eternally contemporaneous with them. He sees in a single eternal moment of comprehension the whole unfolded pattern of each man's life. Therefore, God's determination about us is taken in the light of all that we are and do, and while it is true that he does not deal with us according to our merits or deserts, it is also true that no man is saved against his own settled determination not to be saved. God's grace, powerful and efficacious as it is, must have some opening in the human heart, however small, through which it may enter. The gracious action of God is not in violation of human freedom but rather is welcomed and received as that which makes fuller freedom possible. In any profound human relationship, such as falling in love for example, one is "swept off his feet" but not in a way that seems any violation of his freedom. He wanted to be swept off his feet, and was —perhaps unconsciously—waiting for a long time for it to happen. Freedom and prevenient grace must not be set in opposition to one another. Predestination is simply a way of saying that God, knowing eternally what man will do in his freedom—whether he will resist forever or repent and be saved—respects that freedom and allows each man to "go to his own place"—that dreadfully solemn phrase used of the Apostle Judas. God is not pacing the floor of heaven, wringing his hands in frustration over men who will not—now or ever—repent. He never intended to win any man wholly against that man's will, and the doctrine of Predestination faces that dark possibility quite frankly. This, of course, is not to say who will finally be saved and who will not, but as Calvin pointed out, the daily experience of God's forgiveness and grace and guidance can give a Christian a basis for confidence though not for presumption. This is the kind of fundamental assurance which is produced by "the godly consideration" of Predestination.

CHAPTER EIGHT

The Life of The
World to Come

*T*HE reader of the preceding chapter may feel a sense of letdown at the modesty of our claims for Christian salvation. We have confessed how much of the Christian life is still "lived in the flesh," how little we manifest—either as individuals or as a Church—the distinctive marks of a humanity restored and sanctified in Christ and his Spirit. We have pressed sharp distinctions between a Visible and an Invisible Church, and although we have insisted that the latter is only built up and sanctified in and through the life of the former, it may still leave the reader wondering how Christianity can commend its Gospel to the world if the results of it are so meagre. Sometimes men have defended Christianity on the grounds that "it has never been tried," to which a critic might reply, "What good is a Gospel that after two thousand years has not yet persuaded anyone to try it?" How can the Christian live with this tension between what he has seen in Christ and proclaims as his gift and demand, and what he sees himself and his fellow Christians to be here and now?

The answer is a most uncongenial one to modern thought and

164

has been blunted and avoided by much contemporary heresy as we shall see; it is the promise and expectation of the life of the world to come. One can almost hear critics of Christianity pouncing upon this statement with triumphant cries of vindication of their worst suspicions. "So, it's pie in the sky by and by when you die, after all. Just as we had always thought. Christianity lulls men into acquiescence and complacency and soothes their sense of impatience with promises for the future." Christianity must frankly plead guilty to being an other-world religion. One of the most persistent of our modern heresies has been to deny this by attempting to justify Christianity in terms of its benefits here and now. The nature of these benefits is understood by different apologists in very different ways, but the net result is to try to commend Christianity to the doubtful by showing them what it can do in the present life. "It can help stop Communism" (although Communism has flourished in countries where Christianity has been deeply rooted for centuries); "it can bring peace of mind" (although psychiatrists must often contrive to eliminate religious ideas from their patients' consciousness or subconsciousness before they can be cured); "it builds character and citizenship" (although the normally tolerant Roman Empire found Christians notoriously subversive and malcontent).

The Nature of Our Hope

The unmistakable emphasis of the teaching of the New Testament, on the other hand, is that our hope is not in the present world but in a new world, which although it is breaking into this world in the life of the Christian community is only to be fulfilled and consummated in the future. "If in this life only we have hope," says St. Paul to the Corinthians, "we are of all men the most miserable." As J. B. Phillips has pointed out, modern Christian thought has almost completely reversed the priority of the New Testament. We have sought to justify God, his kingdom, and his grace, by showing how useful he can be in the solution of our earthly problems. The New Testament authors look at things just the other way around. This world, as they see it, is important because it affords opportunities for those decisions, those acts of faith, those commitments which constitute our participation in the life of the eternal kingdom of heaven. The New Testament writer, if he were reflecting on our contemporary scene, would say not that Christianity is useful in combatting Communism, but rather that combatting Communism is useful as a way of expressing our faith in man's destiny of freedom and in demonstrating our commitment to God's purposes of responsible justice and sacrificial love. The Christian view of the future is not some irrelevant addition to the Christian story, a kind of postscript without which the story would nevertheless be whole and intact. If there is no resurrection of the dead then, as St. Paul saw, Christian preaching is empty and Christian faith a mockery.

The consequence of our loss of faith in the life of the world to come is an anxiety and an impatience, a tendency to dogmatize too frantically and to judge too absolutely. In the parable of the tares in the wheat field, Jesus warns men not to try prematurely to separate the weeds from the growing wheat. That discrimination is often difficult, and the uprooting process is often disastrous for the wheat as well as for the weeds. The whole idea of tolerance may very well rest on an understanding of the words of St. Paul, "Judge nothing before the time, until the Lord comes, who will both bring to light the hidden things of darkness and make manifest the counsels of the heart." Only God knows enough about us to make final judgments. Only he who can plumb the counsels of the heart can be trusted in the delicate task of assessing human actions, motives, and character. The very task of distinguishing Christian truth from error (of which this book is a modest example) can only be undertaken with the realization that our best efforts will reflect too much of the perspective of self and of the presuppositions of this world whose wisdom is foolishness with God, and that we must wait for the full vision of his truth until that day when we shall know even as also we are known. Paul Tillich has pointed out the twofold meaning of the recurring biblical command "to wait." [1] To wait means that one both has and does not have. If one had no knowledge whatever of Christian salvation then he could not wait, for he would not know what he was waiting for. On the other hand, if he already possessed the fulness of Christian salvation, there would be no meaning to a command to wait for what is already fully realized. Christian hope consists in the expectation that what we already know and have experienced in part will be crowned and brought to fulfillment. It means both having and not having at the same time. It creates a mood of deep confidence within a tension of almost unbelievable severity. We can bear the burden of the flesh—the sharp struggle within us of our old selves and of the Spirit who is the principle of the new life—because we have a reasonable and holy hope. It is reasonable because we see enough in Christ's resurrection and in our own rescue from despair to know the divine power. It is holy because it has no other ground but the divine mercy and love.

Is this Christian hope a palliative for the creativity of human impatience, an opium which lulls the conscience and deadens the nerve of effort? It is curious that Marxism should have made this criticism of Christianity, for the Communist doctrine might itself be similarly accused. Would it not seem logical that since the Communist dogma about history foresees the inevitable and inescapable victory of the proletariat the predominant mood of the true believers would be one of supine complacency? Why bother stirring up world revolution since it will come inevitably of itself through the inexorable workings of the dialectic of history? This may seem logical. It has not worked out that way in human experience. The assurance that one is a part of "the wave of the future" has more often than not quickened the sense of responsibility and stiffened the sense of purpose and resolution. It may seem paradoxical, but the Calvinists with their strong sense of Providence and Predestination have toiled and fought more zealously than many other Christians. Indeed, one might argue that those who have done most for the world have often been those

---

[1] Cf. the sermon, "Waiting," in *The Shaking of the Foundations* (New York: Scribner's Sons, 1951).

who cared least for the world's rewards and for the world's threats because "they looked for another country, that is an heavenly." Only by a certain kind of detachment from the world can a man find the leverage to lift and save the world. One of the terrible penalties of our current secularism (which really means looking at things only in terms of this world's standards and consequences, for in our sense the word *saecula* means "world") is that we are terribly and anxiously busy in a frantic way which produces little of permanent worth or enduring importance. What could be a better symbol of our loss of the sense of the reality of the world to come than the widespread practice of planned obsolescence whereby things are deliberately produced in such a way that they will not last very long so that we can be busily employed in replacing them? To build with the sense of an eternal judgment on the worth of what we have constructed, whether it be of wood or stone or of straw and rubble, is one of the legacies of an other-worldly Christianity, the loss of which has made our contemporary life so shoddy and cheap and futile.

The mood of Christianity is often likened to that of an army who, although many hard battles remain to be fought, have seen in one decisive encounter where the preponderant power really lies. At some crucial point with all the advantage on his side the enemy has nevertheless been defeated, and so the final issue is no longer really in doubt. This is not an excuse for complacency, but it is an antidote to despair. The resurrection of their Lord seemed to the early Christians to be this kind of encounter, and without it, and the confidence and new principle of life which it released, Christianity would never have been born at all. The mood is not at all one of complacency but rather one of energetic attack inspired by the confidence that no labor is in vain in the Lord. The Christian is not indifferent to the historic consequences of his decisions and actions, but when such consequences are disappointing, when "hopes deceive and fears annoy," the perspective of the world to come enables him to go on doing the wisest and the best he can. St. Paul in a rather complicated passage in I Corinthians (3:11-15) speaks of suffering loss if what he has built in his lifetime is destroyed in the judgment, but, he insists, inasmuch as the foundation which is Christ remains always intact, he himself will be saved. This paradoxical mood of deep involvement in life's dilemmas and ultimate confidence about one's destiny in God's hands has not, of course, always been maintained. Our current danger is to feel fully the tragedies of life but to miss the assurance that even in the worst that can happen God's purpose stands fast and our Christian hope is undismayed. "Troubled on every side yet not in despair" is the way St. Paul describes this characteristic Christian experience.

The Heresy of Progress

This Christian outlook on history lost much of its depth and profundity in the optimism of the nineteenth and twentieth centuries and became distorted into the heresy of progress. Progress is an idea wholly absent from the New Testament. There is no hint in the literature of first-century Christianity that things will become better and better, certainly not that the practice of the Christian ethic will eliminate the power of evil from the world. The New Testament uniformly looked forward to an early termination of the history of "this age" by a climactic intervention of God, and the responsibility of the Christian was not so much to improve the world in general as it was to create a kind of oasis of obedience and faith in the midst of the evil and deterioration. This confidence in the near approach of the "end" dims somewhat in the later New Testament books, but no conception of progress ever makes its appearance. One of the classic attempts to make some room for the idea of progress in history was St. Augustine's *The City of God*. He considers how one ought to understand Chapter 20 of the book of the Revelation, where the devil is bound for a thousand years and then released for a climactic encounter with God's emissaries before his final destruction. What does this thousand year period represent? asks Augustine, and he assumes that it stands for the present time in

which Christ through the Church exercises a restraining and bind-
ing effect on evil. St. Augustine, although he lived in a time of
enormous social upheaval, believed that Christianity could and
ought to help bring about an amelioration of the life of the world.
He speculates about how war, for example, may be somewhat
mitigated in its ferocity by the Christian consideration of the true
aim of war which is to resist injustice and create the conditions
for peace. But St. Augustine's optimism about all this is always
tempered by the knowledge that it does not really eliminate the
root of evil in the world; it does not destroy the devil but only
chains and controls him. St. Augustine's temperate optimism is
the only kind of optimism that is consistent with Christian faith.
It is as far removed from the utopian illusions of much early
twentieth-century religious liberalism as it is from the resignation
and despair over this world held by recurring premillennial sects.[2]
This Christian optimism is a corrective to a spreading despair and
sense of powerlessness with which our own generation confronts
the problems of containing totalitarian tyranny possessed of nuclear weapons of unimaginable destructiveness. The prospects are
not very good, but even if all efforts are fruitless the Christian
whose final confidence is in the life of the world to come will know
that no bravery, no sacrifice, no imaginative undertaking on behalf of the freedom and dignity of men is ever without its ultimate
vindication or its eternal triumph.

After St. Augustine Christian reflection about the life of the
world to come tended to focus more sharply on the fate of indi-

[a] The word "premillennial" represents the belief that we are not living in the
thousand year period (millennium) as Augustine believed but before the
millennium. Instead of the indefinite future which Augustine believed lay
ahead of the world (he interpreted the thousand years to mean a very ex-
tended period of time), premillennialists insist that the events described in
Revelation 20: 1-3 (the chaining of the devil), have not yet occurred but
may do so at any moment. The recurrence of this idea and the resultant
sense of insecurity and uncertainty marks Christian history again and again.
This kind of anticipation only becomes heretical if it indulges in fruitless
speculation about times and seasons, the kind of speculation Jesus warns
his followers against in several places in the Gospels (cf. St. Matthew 24:
36). Unfortunately, most premillennial literature is entirely of this speculative type.

vidual than upon the fate of history as a whole, and the classical medieval view of the future life combined an individual judgment for each person at death with a general resurrection and judgment at the end of history. The importance of the individual and his final fate began to emerge in the Bible itself. The book of Daniel (12:2) speaks of a resurrection of some of the dead—presumably, the conspicuously virtuous who deserve a reward, and the conspicuously wicked who deserve special punishment—and, of course, faith in the resurrection of the dead is held by St. Paul and the other major New Testament writers.

Resurrection *vs.* Immortality

Many readers will already know that this biblical faith in "the Resurrection of the body"—as the Apostles' Creed puts it—is to be carefully distinguished from the philosophical belief in immortality. The latter—which is found in Plato, for example—rests upon a distinction between that which is inherently immortal in man, namely, his soul, and that which is ephemeral and of no ultimate significance, namely, his physical body. Immortality looks upon death as a kind of release of the essentially deathless soul from the restricting and imprisoning body. The resurrection doctrine of the New Testament, however, knows of no such deathless part of man and does not at all make the assumption that anything human is exempt from the penalty of death. "Man that is born of woman hath but a short time to live; he cometh up and is cut down like a flower and never continueth in one stay. In the midst of life we are in death." There is no hint in sober biblical words like those that some core of the human self is immune from death's rigorous sentence. Immortality may be true, but whether it is or not does not matter to the Christian whose faith is not at all in the survival of some part of the self after death, but in the reconstitution by God of a full and complete human personality at the general resurrection.

Resurrection is obviously an idea more congenial to the Christian doctrine of man and creation than immortality is. Resurrection means that every aspect of human personality has potential significance and a share in the glorification of the self which awaits every man who is ready to receive it. Resurrection proclaims the essential interdependence of body, soul, and spirit in the make-up of a human person. A disembodied spirit is a welcome idea in Greek thought, where the body and material existence are a hindrance to fulness of life, but to Christian thought a disembodied spirit is a tragic shadow of real life, a truncated and only half-alive being, as frustrated as a violinist without any violin through which to express his love of music. As we saw in thinking about creation and the doctrine of man, persons are inconceivable apart from some organism, some body, through which self-expression can be realized. A parishioner of the author once objected to the phrase, "the Resurrection of the body," in the creed. She was an intense and vital person but had suffered a severe attack of polio in childhood which left her legs badly crippled. "I do not want to think," she protested, "of dragging these crippled legs all through eternity." The answer to that objection was hard for her to understand, but the truth was that no one of us who knew her would recognize her apart from the triumphant and brave way she had surmounted her afflictions and transmuted her limitations into just one more facet of a generous and sympathetic personality. In the resurrection one can be sure that the pain and frustration will all be gone, but there will yet remain some marks of what she has suffered, for apart from such marks she would not really be her full self. It does not seem irreverent to compare such physical limitations—yes, and psychological limitations too—to the scars which were manifest in the glorified body of the risen Christ. "He showed unto them his hands and his side." Of course he did, for how else should they have known him? He carried into glory the limitations with which he had been beset in this life. He did not just rise above them and forget them. He triumphed not in spite of them but in and through them.

Resurrection also underlines the everlasting significance of the individual personality. There is a subtle danger in some modern funeral practices of blunting the force of this proclamation, especially in the substitution of "memorial services" for the traditional service of the Burial of the Dead. The memorial service lays its emphasis primarily on the kind of immortality which is attained by influencing and making one's contribution to the life and welfare of mankind. "We live on in the hearts and lives of those who knew us and loved us." One trusts that this is so, although human memory is not always as keen as we should like it to be. A non-Christian faculty member in one of our universities once protested at the shocking implications of some lines in the hymn, "O God, Our Help in Ages Past." "How inappropriate it is," he complained, "to have to sing 'Time like an ever rolling stream/ Bears all its sons away;/ They fly, forgotten, as a dream/ Dies at the opening day.' Surely we do not want to be reminded at a memorial service of the shortness and uncertainty of our memories of the departed." The hymn, of course, is more realistic than the professor, whose hope lay in an immortality of influence. That theory may comfort the prominent and influential; it has little to say to those who recognize themselves in the description in Ecclesiasticus: "Some there be that have no memorial, who are perished as though they had never been."

What is more serious, immortality by influence puts the premium on the outward performance and the impact it makes on the outside world. The most vivid immortality is reserved for those who make the biggest impression on their contemporaries, who are most often in the headlines, whose public relations were the most efficient and effective. The Christian doctrine of the resurrection, on the other hand, commends each one of us to the final judgment of God, who will know of inner triumphs and secret victories which were entirely hidden from the world and consequently did very little to influence or enrich it. Whatever benefits flow from a human life are a cause of thanksgiving to the God who inspired so much of it, but they are not the ground of our Christian hope. The mercy and the power of God, of the God "unto whom all hearts are open, all desires known, and from whom no secrets are hid," are the sources of our Christian belief that each person, no matter how obscure in the world's eyes, counts with God and receives from him the crown and fulfillment of his life.

Judgment, Heaven, and Hell

These convictions are expressed in the classical doctrines of the last judgment, heaven, and hell. Because they have suffered distortions and misunderstanding they are often overlooked in our contemporary Christian teaching and preaching, and in order to restore them to their place in the balance of Christian orthodoxy we shall need to resolve some of the problems they raise for modern thought. One of these problems is that this whole section of Christian doctrine seems to intrude the low motives of rewards and punishments into what ought to be the quite selfless and idealistic pursuit of the Christian life. But if this is indeed an intrusion of low motives, it appears to have begun as early as the recorded teachings of Jesus himself. At the end of the Sermon on the Mount as found in the Gospels of St. Matthew and St. Luke —a sermon where the motive for Christian ethical life and action is declared to be the imitation and response to the love and mercy of the Father and the desire to be his sons—the promise and threat of the story of the two houses, one built on the rock and the other on the sand, give the sermon a final note of reward and punishment which may seem inconsistent in tone and spirit with much which has preceded it. But Amos Wilder has suggested [3] that anticipation of rewards and punishments is not held out by Jesus as the *motive* of ethics so much as it is set forth as a solemn reminder of the *consequences* of obedience or disobedience. Any college instructor seeks to create as the motive in his students a love of truth and a passion for accuracy and clarity of perception, but he is derelict in his duty if he does not also point out the sombre consequences in the Dean's office of a failure to complete

[3] See his *Eschatology and Ethics in the Teachings of Jesus* (New York: Harper and Brothers, 1939), for a fuller treatment of this seeming inconsistency.

the prescribed requirements of the course. The student ought to work for the love of knowledge; but if this high motive fails to operate effectively, there are certain practical consequences which it is only fair to point out. Similarly the Christian is called to live out the demands of the Sermon on the Mount for the sake of the love he bears to God, but if he ignores this summons it is legitimate to point out that he is incurring the serious penalty of missing the chief joy and satisfaction of life and that has the most serious eternal consequences.

This leads to a second consideration, and that is that the joys of heaven and the sufferings of hell are entirely consistent with the aims and ideals of those who are assigned these two differing destinies. C. S. Lewis in one of his most successful books, *The Great Divorce,* gives a vivid picture of hell as the abode of the self-centered and heaven as the abode of those whose life has found its center in the glory and reality of God. To the self-centered the blazing glory of God is an intolerable light from which they shrink, and his reality and power a firm and unyielding structure which they find harsh and rough. Although a bus goes every day from hell to heaven and although anyone who wants to may take the trip—and indeed may remain in heaven if he wishes— almost no one takes advantage of the offer, for the inhabitants of hell are where they want to be and where they belong, and it is part of God's mercies that they are permitted to live where they may shield themselves from his radiance and brilliance. As Mr. Lewis points out, the classical descriptions of heaven—hosts of the redeemed endlessly praising and adoring the majesty of God —have little appeal to the ordinary non-Christian, who avoids even an hour of such an occupation on Sunday mornings here on earth. There is nothing low and unworthy about *some* of the rewards men seek. Is it demeaning for a musician to seek the rewards of producing great music? The answer would surely be "no," although it would be demeaning to seek a reward such as a lot of money or the satisfaction of being a celebrity. Christianity's rewards are not "pie in the sky" but the full vision and knowledge of God forever and ever.

One of the most alarming things Jesus ever said is, "They have their reward." He was talking about people who were religious for the wrong reasons. They gave alms to salve their consciences and prayed to establish a reputation for piety. Broadly speaking, however, Jesus' words mean more than that; they mean that a man has as his eternal destiny whatever he sets his heart on. If he sets his heart on himself, he can live for himself for all eternity. If he sets his heart on God, he can live for God for all eternity. The doctrine of heaven and hell pay this ultimate tribute to man's freedom—God will respect human integrity throughout all eternity and if a man insists on rejecting God's offers of mercy and of love, then he must live outside their influence. To deny the possibility of hell is to misunderstand altogether God's ways with man. He never violates human integrity. He is a God who hides himself in order that men may be free—if they wish—to flout his laws and reject his grace, yes, even to deny his reality and power. It is incongruous with all we know about God to suppose that at the last moment he will abandon his determination and force men into heaven against their wills. Hell is a possibility if man is really free. We do not know its population statistics, but we know that it is there for those who choose it.

Judgment *vs.* Justification

There remains a final difficulty with the doctrines of heaven and hell and that is how they are to be made consistent with the idea of justification by faith. As we saw in our consideration of salvation, God accepts us and receives and acknowledges us as his sons entirely apart from any merit or deserving on our part. Is it possible to suppose that the God who is so generous and overflowing in love and mercy will finally reverse his character and begin parcelling out rewards and punishments like a judge in a law court? In the language of the courts, we are declared acquitted by Christ. "Who is he that condemneth," asks St. Paul, and it is scarcely conceivable that the answer is "God himself at the last judgment!" How can the boundless love of God, which is the heart of the Gospel, be made consistent with a God of justice who presides at the day of judgment? Faced with this problem, popular thinking has given up the idea of judgment altogether and concluded that the transition into heaven is automatically guaranteed for every one by the doctrine of the divine mercy and forgiveness. The consequences of this heresy have been to relax the tension of the Christian commandments and to cheapen the value of the Christian promises.

Judgment is not, however, inconsistent with love and mercy, if the love and mercy have as their goal the development of personality in all its fulness and dignity. Judgment is the reverse side of love, for real love sets a standard for the beloved and holds him to it with a fierceness that a sense of impersonal justice would never generate. Even the divine mercy must take into account the stubborn fact that in some instances every offer of forgiveness is rejected and every appeal of love is trampled upon and denied. Divine love is not mere indulgence; it is the burning passion of the heart of God that man shall achieve the dignity of his creation and that if in his freedom he rejects this destiny, he shall be made to see what he has done. Judgment in a law court is not primarily punishment but the discovery of the truth. Kierkegaard compared the last judgment to the unmasking which takes place at midnight at a masked ball. We shall see what we are and what we have been. The nations assembled before the judgment seat in St. Matthew's parable of the sheep and the goats protested that they did not know that in neglecting Christ's needy and suffering brethren they were neglecting him. That is what the judgment is intended to show us—the meaning of what we have done and left undone. If we have refused mercy, and flouted love, and trampled upon forgiveness, then even God cannot draw us to himself against our will, and we must accept the consequences of our freedom.

No one may anticipate this judgment of God. The modern tendency to be agnostic about the ultimate fate of an individual— no matter how bitter and selfish and evil he has seemed to be— is a necessary corollary of our conviction that only God knows enough to judge any one's ultimate destiny and fate. The smugness of some churches' conviction that failure to make certain theological affirmations or to perform certain sacramental acts damns a man for eternity is simply contradictory to every analogy of human love and sympathy which Christians have used to picture God and his love for men. The doctrine of Christ's sacrificial death has already shown us how far out on the road of reconciliation the Father is ready to go if by any means men may be saved. Judgment by such a compassionate Christ is not something to be despaired of but something to brace and challenge us, who in our better moments really do want to see ourselves as we are, however painful and humiliating that vision may be.

The Heresy of Spiritualism

Despite all this Christian tradition about the ultimate fate and destiny of human beings, our natural love and concern prompt us to ask additional questions: "What is happening to the dead now? Where are they and do they know and pray for us? Are they still progressing in the Christian life or are they at rest or asleep?" In many cases the urgency of these questions has led to a resort to spiritualism and other forms of psychic experimentation. Christian orthodoxy objects to spiritualism, not, of course, on the ground that it is impossible (although the evidence will seem inconclusive to the objective enquirer) but on the ground that, if true, it is an abuse of a human personality (the so-called medium, who becomes the unconscious tool of the departed), and that it degrades and cheapens the relationship between the Church on earth and the Church at rest. It is difficult to believe that real love and trust need to be reinforced by table-thumpings and mysterious cabalistic communication which remains so unsatisfactory and so fragmentary. If the methods of spiritualism were intended to be the normal means of communication between the dead and the living then surely that communication would be fuller, clearer, and more profoundly moving and satisfying than is the case in the reports one usually receives of alleged conversations. The recurring popularity of spiritualism and of psychic investigation shows how insecure is our faith in God's power and love. We snatch at absurd bits of supposed evidence for justification of a faith which ought to rest on the knowledge of Christ's resurrection and on a trust in his promise, "that where I am, there ye may be also."

The Defective Doctrine of Purgatory

The present state of the departed is not a subject on which speculation is likely to be very profitable, and it is certainly not an area where dogmatic definition is appropriate. Two extreme views seem ruled out by our Christian experience. One is the Roman Catholic doctrine of purgatory. It pictures the life of the intermediate state—as it is usually called—in which most of the dead now find themselves as entirely punitive in character, where the punishments due each man's sin must be worked off as a prelude to the entry into heaven. This process may be speeded up by the intercession of others and by their performance of certain meritorious acts which can be applied toward the remission of the penalties still outstanding against the departed. Such a picture of God as a public accountant is wholly inconsistent with the Christian Gospel, and the transference of merit implies that there is something deficient in the merits of our Lord's death and passion, which alone are the source of the Christian's confidence about the future life.

The Two Stages in Salvation

This is not to say that the opposite view, usually characterizing Protestant thought which was in understandable reaction to the Roman doctrine, is adequate either. According to this view the eternal destiny of the individual is once for all determined at death, and his passage to heaven needs no preparatory or intermediary stage at all. But this overlooks the fact that there are two stages in salvation. One is the initial assurance, the new confidence, the birth of a new relationship to God wherein we know ourselves to be pardoned and accepted by him despite all our shortcomings and all our rebellion and sin. As we have seen, this first step is what is usually called justification. While it is never left behind—for we never, even in the life of the world to come, are without the need of the divine mercy—justification leads to what we have called with Kierkegaard "endless striving born of gratitude." The question is: does this "endless striving" end with death or does it continue in a new way and on a new level of human existence? Although we know little about this, logic seems to require us to say that there must be development in sanctification, as it is called, beyond death. The penitent thief at the Cross, although he was accepted and forgiven by the dying Christ, had much to learn and to become before he could be at home in the kingdom or in the companionship of this royal person who welcomed and received him. And what shall we say of those who never had an opportunity for one reason or another truly to hear the Gospel or freely to receive it? There are not many people in the world 2000 years after the apostles were set the task of going to the uttermost parts of the earth who have never heard of the Gospel with their outward ears, but how many there are—certainly on a modern college campus—who have known only such a perverted and corrupted Gospel that they have quite justifiably shut their ears to any Christian preaching at all. Even more pressing is the question of defective and subnormal persons whose freedom and reason were never sufficiently developed in this life to make any responsible hearing of the story of Christ a real possibility. Development after death is not discussed in the New Testament, but all we know about God's mercy and our own desire to be like him at his appearing lead us to suppose that death does not end our striving and that we who remain are knit together with the departed in a fellowship of developing and deepening devotion supported by mutual prayer and expressed most fully in common praise and adoration. "Therefore with Angels and Archangels, and with all the company of heaven, we laud and magnify thy glorious Name; evermore praising thee and saying, Holy, Holy, Holy."

The Divine Purpose Fulfilled

"Then cometh the end." There will be a time, a time which is no longer time at all but an everlasting moment of utter fulfillment and complete joy, in which the striving finally will cease and the perfection of the divine purpose will everywhere be realized. Christian writers have stumbled and stammered as they sought to picture what this final bliss of heaven would be like. Harps, crowns, palms, incense, wings, precious stones and golden streets, all of this imagery is but the poor effort of the human mind to describe a realization of all its dreams and hopes. If it does not stir the minds of contemporary Christians, then our poets must give us more glorious pictures for our own time, for heaven is the everlasting fulfillment of every high moment of truth and beauty and goodness that we have ever known in this life. All our yearning to love and share with one another will there be realized in a mutuality that cannot now even be conceived. At the center of it all will be the divine Love and the divine Energy himself, radiant and glorious beyond anything we have ever known, pouring forth his love into our fully responsive and fully obedient hearts, for he is the answer to all our striving and the satisfaction of all our desires, and so we shall be at rest finally in him and with one another in the kingdom of his love. Apart from this faith one must conclude that life is bitterly frustrating and tantalizingly meaningless. The yearning in our hearts for reality, for purity, for love, yearning which only begins to be satisfied within the span of this life, is a mockery and a delusion if there is never to be any completion of the quest to which it calls us.

If there is any purpose in life at all, then the kind of hopes that man discovers in the deepest part of his being have a meaning, are intended to be fulfilled, were planted that some day they might flower and bear their fruit. Every man must have some satisfying picture of what the end of all our striving is to be if the striving is not to be touched with cynicism and finally paralyzed by despair. Christianity sees the end as a fulfillment of those qualities which are most deeply personal and individual and yet which bind men most strongly and indissolubly together—trust in God and love for our fellows. Heaven is the culmination of every act of courage and integrity where the self stood up alone and said, "I believe." Heaven is the fulfillment of every effort to share life with our fellows, to enter into their joys, and to knit our purposes with theirs. To lose this vision, as our generation has so largely done, means that we have nothing superlative and glorious to serve or to hope for, and life peters out in futility, resignation, and terrible weariness. Our modern heresy, which declares that this life is enough, frames human existence too narrowly and too meanly, and nullifies all the great hopes by which men have lived and for which they have died. By its affirmation of faith in the life of the world to come, Christianity is not pretending to foresee in detail what in the very nature of things can never be very clearly known or described; it is simply declaring, against the sentence of futility which death passes, that the noblest ambitions of the race are not foolishness and vanity but have their reward. This is the capstone of Christian orthodoxy; this is the final certification of the validity of the whole Christian experience of salvation. Just because it is so indescribable and so inconceivable, this faith in the life of the world to come is the ultimate proof that Christianity is a trust and a faith and a life-adventure in which the things that can be proved in cold logic or by the test of the senses must be left behind, and that we go out not knowing whither we go, sure of only one thing—that the kind of life that was in Christ will have its crown and its reward and that all we have known of his mercy emboldens us to trust him to bring us to that kind of life and to share it with us forever and ever.